Boom & Bust: Ecuador's Financial Rollercoaster

The Interplay between Finance, Politics and Social Conditions in 20th century Ecuador

Pablo R. Izurieta Andrade

Vernon Press

www.vernonpress.com

In the Americas:
Vernon Press
1000 N West Street,
Suite 1200, Wilmington,
Delaware 19801
United States

In the rest of the world
Vernon Press
C/Sancti Espiritu 17,
Malaga, 29006
Spain

Library of Congress Control Number: 2015942450

ISBN: 978-1-62273-470-2

Synopsis

This work proposes a connection of financial circumstances with major socio-political events in 20th-century Ecuador. It highlights the state of the nation's economy as a determinant factor in the outcome of events. Throughout the history of Ecuador, the ambivalent evolution of major political and social events such as the stability of serving presidents, coups and war, has had an interesting and direct relationship to the financial environment. If the economy was healthy, did the country also experience stability? If it went into disarray, did the non-financial environment follow? Data collected from the Central Bank of Ecuador, unpublished diplomatic papers, and personal documents from relevant historical figures, as well as from the work of previous historians, indicate a strong effect of financial and economic performance on major political and social events. Particularly, given the country's dependence on three main commodities: cacao, bananas and oil, the performance of these significantly shaped 20th-century Ecuadorian history.

To my mother and grandmother

Acknowledgements

I would like to acknowledge all the people who in one way or another helped me complete this book. Mention is needed for my family, whose support has allowed me to complete this work, especially my grandmother, mother, and uncle. I would also like to acknowledge all the people at the different universities that have aided me in the research, especially Professor Candelaria Garay at Harvard University for all her wonderful support.

Table of Contents

List of Tables

List of Pictures

Introduction

Every nation on Earth is shaped by major social and political events. Government collapses, a coup d'état, war, social unrest are all examples of what constitutes a major sociopolitical event. Some events are more transcendental than others, and some seem to shift the course of history altogether. In the South American nation of Ecuador, these undeniably include the Liberal Revolution of 1895, the Julian Revolution of 1925, the wars with Peru, and the continuous ousting of presidents. But what caused these events? Was it strong intellectual ideals? Political motivations? Or is there an economically motivated explanation?

Take Ecuador's ratification of the Río Protocol (a major event). American oil companies, through the United States government, pressured Ecuador into signing the Rio Protocol, effectively relinquishing over 200,000 km^2 of territory to Peru, says Jorge Villacres, a renowned historian, in *Problemas Económicos y Políticos del Ecuador.* He suggests that the United States had an agreement with the Peruvian government to make use of the perceived oil in the disputed territories. Or was it, as the traditional argument goes, that the United States pressured Ecuador because it wanted a united continent against the Axis powers in the midst of World War II. Was it idealism, political motivations, or dollars and cents?

The underlying importance of economic performance in Ecuadorian historical events is frequently sidelined. Often, the economy is a subject on its own but rarely is it used as an explanation for major events. Historians have focused on the ups and downs of the economy, on the success and failures of economic policy, on commerce, and have made a case within these focus points. They have focused on a variety of subjects such as the history of Ecuador's main financial groups, and the impact of oil in the economy. But the connection between economic performance and major sociopolitical events has often been relegated from a major issue. Moreover, Ecuadorian historiography has frequently favored political and ethnographic explanations, which is why an outlook weighing in economic performance should be welcomed as a different and valid point of view. It is not the intention of this book to enter into specific debates about what is it that decides history, but rather to demonstrate the continuous connection between financial struggles and revolt, production stability with order, and the other directions history takes as a result of economic circumstances. Through the examination of historical documents and statistics, including relevant financial an economic indicators, this work shows the strong connection that exists.

The pattern that emerges time and time again between major sociopolitical events and their economical fundamentals cannot be overlooked. Oil was discovered by Standard Oil's exploration in the Ecuadorian *oriente* region, yet its significance lies in the change it brought to Ecuadorian life through the influx of vast amounts of money into the country. Petroleum was one of three commodities that experienced booms throughout the 20th century; the other two are cacao and bananas, which became integral to the country's health. Being a country dependent on one of these three single products for every growth spree in one hundred years, the performance of these commodity industries was pivotal in modeling the events that shaped Ecuador's history. As such, the bonanzas of cacao, bananas, and oil should have been fundamental causes of change in Ecuadorian history and ought to be included in connection with the major events of 20th-century Ecuador.

This pattern is clear throughout Ecuador's history. Located on the Pacific coast of South America, between Colombia and Peru, Ecuador came into existence in 1830 after the dissolution of what has come to be known as *La Gran Colombia* (the Great Colombia), which under Spanish rule was known as the Viceroyalty of Nueva Granada. The three departments of the South (Guayas, Cuenca & Quito) decided on May 13, 1830, to separate from Colombia and form a new sovereign state. On the first article of its constitution, the three departments of the south stated their intention to form a single body, which would assume the name *Republic of Ecuador*, and thus relinquishing the traditional and historic name of Quito, which had been in place since the 16th century.

Just as it would happen throughout the following century, the dawn of this new republic would be affected by instability, fueled largely by financial stress. The nation's first president, Juan Jose Flores, took office in the least favorable of conditions. Ecuador's army was disproportionately large, there was internal disunion, the country still had not established precise borders with Colombia or Peru, and sovereignty was relative as, technically, Ecuador was still part of Colombia. At its birth, the country faced three main concerns: international recognition of its sovereignty, border disputes, and the inclusion of the territories of Cauca (present-day Colombia), which had been part of the province of

Quito but were being held by two rogue Generals who wanted to create their own separate state in them. Regarding international recognition of sovereignty, Ecuador was quick to receive support from Peru and Bolivia. However, this recognition was not necessarily a gesture of friendship, but rather, in the case of Peru, a result of a standing resentment towards Colombia, as well as part of a cunning strategy to invade Ecuador as Peru knew that it could defeat the Ecuadorian army but not the Colombian.

Map of Ecuador and its neighbors

Source: Free Open Source Portable Atlas (http://ian.macky.net/pat/map/ec/ec.html)

In this context, the country simply could not afford to satisfy everybody's unsettled sentiments and ended up with a string of uprisings by soldiers who demanded pay. With over half the new nation's budget already going to supporting the military, these uprisings could not be suppressed. And thus, at the dawn of the Republic, its financial problems resulted in terrible consequences. Cauca ended within the new Colombian territory. Peru, from then up until the late 20th century, continuously invaded and took gigantic parts of what had been the department of Quito during Gran Colombia. And as Ecuador's history demonstrates, the root of this problem would not be solved for the following 170 years after the nation's founding.

Ever since the Quito rebellion of 1809, one the earliest movements for independence in South America (hence the name, *Quito, Luz de América,* Light of America), the decades of continued political instability have been accompanied by continued depression and debt. Similarly, the decades of stability and progress have been accompanied by financial prosperity usually spearheaded by a high-yielding export commodity. During the 19th century, Ecuador's rural economy predominantly depended on the cultivation of cash crops and inexpensive raw materials that were in turn dependent on world markets. Thus, just like the patterns that would define the 20th century, Ecuador in the 19th century was characterized by upsetting unpredictability.

This work tries to explain Ecuador's major sociopolitical events across the 20th century through the lenses of changing financial and economic circumstances. The circumstances surrounding the most transcendental events in 20th-century Ecuador, including the three biggest commodity booms that shaped the country's fate, will be analyzed and connected to the nation's major events. The story begins in 1895, at the dawn of the liberal revolution. A time of clamored change, where one of Ecuador's most prominent personalities was the head of state, and where the cacao bonanza would determine the form the country would take. Ecuador's history will take us through the age of crises, the dawn of the banana republic, and through to the oil era culminating in a fantastic implosion at the dawn of the new millennium.

Chapter 1

The Liberal Era (1895-1925)

In the 1860s a riveting idea struck the Swiss, they combined chocolate with milk. Previously, cacao was used to produce a bitter hot beverage that not everybody wanted to indulge in. Its taste was certainly an acquired one, and its high price tag made it a luxury few would try to obtain. Yet this spectacular Swiss idea changed all of this when they created one of the most beloved foods in the world. All of a sudden everyone wanted chocolate. In Britain, net imports of "cocoa" increased by a factor of eight, and the annual per capita consumption of it surpassed that of the nation's preferred beverage, tea.[1] In the United States alone, the number of chocolate factories increased from 949 in 1869 to 2,391 in 1914,[2] and Ecuador was the place where all these ever-growing producers could get their essential ingredient, cacao.

Quickly, Ecuador became the world's superpower in cacao production. The soaring demand for chocolate rose Ecuadorian cacao exports 700% from the 1870s to the 1920s making cacao the leading Ecuadorian export by far, representing three-fourths of all exportations (see table 1). This brought an age of transformation to the country. Government was able to acquire stability principally through the increasing influx of state revenue due to the cacao trade. Controversial projects could be implemented, useful or not as these may have been, without a fallout of the administration. As it happened, society became organized around the cacao trade, and as such, Ecuador's destiny in the first decades of the 20th century would be the result of how this product would be managed. Essentially, the evolution of the cacao trade fundamentally affected the political dynamics of the country because it was the critical component of state revenue and the Ecuadorian economy.

---

1 Paul Henderson, "Cocoa, Finance and the State in Ecuador, 1895-1925," *Bulletin of Latin American Research* 16 (1997): 171.

2 Ronn Pineo, *Ecuador and the United States: Useful Strangers (The United States and the Americas)* (Athens: University of Georgia Press, 2007), Kindle Edition, 747.

Table 1: Ecuadorian Cacao Exports, 1900-1925[3]

Year	Kilos (100s)	Value (1000s sucres)	Value (1000s $)	% of total exports
1900	18,791	10,908	5321	70.7
1901	23,179	12,255	6007	74.8
1902	24,398	13,231	6583	73.1
1903	23,005	12,195	6128	65.5
1904	28,564	15,249	7780	65.5
1905	21,127	10,916	5656	58.7
1906	23,426	12,198	6386	55.5
1907	19,703	13,478	6543	58.8
1908	32,119	17,737	8250	66.8
1909	31,570	14,523	6982	58.4
1910	36,305	16,214	7721	57.8
1911	38,803	16,095	8088	61.3
1912	38,225	15,716	7413	55.8
1913	41,869	20,524	9546	63.2
1914	47,210	20,769	9985	77.3
1915	37,019	19,938	8981	75.1
1916	42,667	26,236	11,309	72.6
1917	45,193	21,947	8779	65.4
1918	38,416	17,116	7102	62.2
1919	44,680	29,491	13,911	68.2
1920	39,790	35,573	15,810	71.3
1921	40,709	20,363	5518	60.0
1922	40,361	30,241	7287	65.6
1923	29,564	18,890	4971	49.2
1924	30,505	32,240	6072	49.4
1925	32,281	33,986	7742	46.2

Financial Stability, Investment, Infrastructure & Reform

The liberal era was a period in Ecuadorian history marked by a deep change in social policy. It came to fruition in response to a string of conservative and religious governments that advocated a strict social and Catholic-based policy in all matters of Ecuadorian life. It was spearheaded by Ecuadorian general and two-times president Eloy Alfaro (1895-1901, 1906-1911), and came at a time when cacao dominated the Ecuadorian economy. This enabled the new liberal government to enact reforms that have been popularized in many Ecuadorian history schoolbooks for

[3] Henderson, "Cocoa, Finance and the State in Ecuador, 1895-1925," 173

decades. Some of these revolutionary reforms include the strict separation of church and state, growth of public education, civil marriages and divorce, and laic education. In earnest, Alfaro's push for secular education reform is perhaps the greatest legacy from this celebrated Ecuadorian president as he also dwelled in other endeavors that are somewhat more controversial.

One such contentious endeavor is the Guayaquil-Quito railroad. This, another project that has been popularized in Ecuadorian history and folklore, seems at a glance as a magnificent project to unite a country that has, throughout its history, been divided both culturally and geographically between the coast and the sierra regions. Transportation between the two biggest cities, Quito, the capital in the highlands, to Guayaquil, the nation's most important seaport, was outlandish. As it was at the beginning of the 20th-century, shipping a ton of wheat between these two cities was more expensive than from Australia to Europe.[4]

Supported by the United States, the railroad generated great expectations. It was hoped, as the United States consul to Ecuador at the time would state, "prove a blessing to Ecuador in every conceivable respect."[5] Yet contrary to expectations, Alfaro ignored the fact that a railroad of the characteristics required to connect Quito and Guayaquil was astronomically expensive and quite difficult to build. The idea was grandiose, but its implementation was complicated and unprepared. A contract was drafted in which Alfaro's personal acquaintance, Archer Harman, agreed to make Alfaro's *Obra Redentora*,[6] the railroad, a reality.

The cost for Ecuador to build the railroad was set at $17,532,000[7] (which would amount to about $493,348,160 in 2015 dollars). But before Ecuador could issue new bonds to raise that amount, the country had to arrange a solution for its existing foreign debt. Existing since the days of

---

4 Pineo, *Useful Strangers*, 871

5 Pineo, *Useful Strangers*, 877

6 *Obra Redentora*, redemptive work. Alfaro believed that the railroad would give Ecuador economic, political and even spiritual salvation.

7 Pineo, *Useful Strangers*, 888

independence, Ecuador had continuously[8] failed to service this debt[9] and thus had to somehow satisfy its principal creditor, the British Council for Foreign Bondholders, before new bonds could be issued for railway construction. After tortuous handling of the new bonds, and with the agreements on the old debt,[10] and the many complications regarding the actual construction that started from day one, a solution was reached in which the British financed a U.S. company (led by Harman) to build the Ecuadorian railroad. This all seemed possible because of the financial security brought about by the cacao trade. As a matter of fact this was very much the case because if profits from the railroad ever fell short, it was finally agreed, the Ecuadorian government would guarantee the service of the new debt through the revenue collected at the Guayaquil customs house. In essence, Ecuador pledged the continuously increasing funds that were being collected through the cacao trade. As income from cacao exports largely determined the levels of imports, the tax collected on incoming goods (as well as through the export tax) represented a major source of ordinary state revenue.[11]

The cacao trade, or *la pepa de oro*[12], as the cacao bean would eventually become known, introduced dramatic changes. Not only did it make a massive project like the Ecuadorian railroad a reality, every citizen was affected in one way or another. Ecuador, as a result of cacao, was integrated into the world economy and optimism was abundant. Even the British Chargé d' Affaires in Quito stated, during the problematical first

---

[8] Between 1834 and 1898, Ecuador was in default for 53 years. Linda Alexander Rodriguez, *The Search for Public Policy: Regional Politics and Government Finances in Ecuador, 1830-1940* (Berkeley: University of California Press, 1985), 108.

[9] Commonly known as the *English Debt.*

[10] Harman reached an accord with the bondholders entailing a 70% diminution of the debt: "each 100 pounds of consolidated debt bonds with accrued interest were exchanged for 36 pounds of First Mortgage Bonds of the Guayaquil and Quito Railway, bearing 6% interest and redeemable at 1% per year, and a cash bonus of 2 pounds 10 shillings." Rodriguez, *Government Finances and the Search for Public Policy.*

[11] Guayaquil customhouse receipts accounted for 70%-80% of all tax revenues collected between 1895-1914 (Ronn Pineo, *Useful Strangers,* 786).

[12] The golden bean.

months of World War I, that Ecuador "if properly administered...would be the richest of the West Coast South American States."[13]

Yet the newfound wealth did not do much to change the status quo and the inequalities that existed in the country. If anything, one could argue, it deepened them. Since colonial times, the economic and social structure that existed in Ecuador was built around *haciendas*. These gigantic lands and their owners, the *hacendados*, dictated the route of the nation's economy, and with the coming of cacao this structure hardly changed. The most obvious example of the hacienda system is that of the Caamaño family's[14] *Hacienda Tenguel.*[15] This 100,000 hectares property extended from the pacific coast up to the edge of the Andes, and during the Cacao boom, Tenguel had a plantation of 3 million cacao trees that in 1921 produced 30,626[16] out of the 40,709 quintales[17] that the entire country generated, a staggering 75.2% of all cacao production. This also meant that Tenguel's cacao production alone constituted over 45% of the country's total exports that year. Other elites included post-independence immigrant families that acquired their estates after 1870. Among the most prominent of these was the Aspiazu family of Basque origin, who together with the Morla and Seminario family became dominant in the Cacao trade. In the case of the latter, with 2 million trees planted, visitors to their lands hailed them as the "cocoa kings of the world."[18]

The control of cacao production by this small nucleus of planter elites permitted these families to become influential in other areas of economic and political activity. A commercial guide to Ecuador from 1909[19] reveals that Lautaro Aspiazu served as director of the *Banco del Ecuador* as well as

---

[13] Henderson, "Cocoa, Finance and the State in Ecuador, 1895-1925," 169.

[14] Ecuadorian president (1883-1888) José María Plácido Caamaño was part of the Caamaño family that owned Hacienda Tenguel.

[15] Since 1910, officially *Caamaño Tenguel Estate Limited.* A British-based-and-backed corporation.

[16] Steve Striffler, *In the Shadows of State and Capital: The United Fruit Company, Popular Struggle, and Agrarian Restructuring in Ecuador, 1900-1995.* (Durham, NC: Duke University Press, 2002), 23.

[17] Quintal: measure equaling 100 kilograms or 220 pounds.

[18] Henderson, "Cocoa, Finance and the State in Ecuador," 174.

[19] Henderson, "Cocoa, Finance and the State in Ecuador," 174.

having a seat in the boards of the most important companies involved in insurance, construction, telephones, lighting, matches, among others. Similarly, the head of the Seminario family also possessed a comparable portfolio of positions, yet it was in the *Banco Comercial y Agrícola* where most of the cacao-elite families converged and exerted their greatest influence (see table 2).

Table 2: Business Interests of Principal Members of the Ecuadorian Exporting/Banking Elite in the Early 20th-century[20]

Large landowning families	Agricultural properties	Export houses	Banco Comercial y Agrícola[a]	Banco del Ecuador[b]	Industries and services[c]
Aspiazu	59	2	26	19	6
Durán Ballén	6	--	19	5	--
Morla	27	--	71	--	1
Seminario	40	1	20	4	3
Puga	17	--	--	--	--
Guzmán	--	1	--	33	1
Caamaño	1	1	--	--	1
Sánchez Bruno	4	--	33	5	--
Reyre	--	1	24	--	1
Parodi	6	--	4	--	--
Avilés	16	--	9	--	2
Díaz Erazo	1	--	28	5	--
Icaza Illingworth	9	--	10	6	1
Ribón	--	--	12	--	--
Sáenza de Tejada	2	--	11	--	--
Osa	--	--	20	--	--

Note: [a]Number of shares of 5000 sucres; [b]Number of shares of 8000 sucres; [c]Number of firms in which interests held.

These influences however, were not at center stage during the first years of the Liberal era in Ecuador. During this time, the Ecuadorian government was concerned with the building of infrastructure, of which the railroad was of highest importance. The construction of the railroad, which was completed in 1908[21], was built during the stable governments of Alfaro and Leonidas Plaza (1901-1905, 1912-1916). After Plaza's presidency culminated in 1905, the vice-president, Lizardo Garcia, ran for

[20] Henderson, "Cocoa, Finance and the State in Ecuador," 175.

[21] It is worth mentioning that the railroad was a failure, Harman was paid to build a "first-class" railway but actually built a very sub-standard one. Costs soared out of control, and over five hundred workers died of small pox and other diseases. The railroad became a source of frustration and problems and not the salvation Alfaro had hoped for.

office and easily won the electoral process. It was not until *El Viejo luchador*[22] decided that the liberal revolution needed him as leader again that things would sway. He deposed president Garcia in 1906, after only less than five months in office.

Aside from the Alfaro-provoked exchanges of power, the liberal era of the early 20th-century was a time of visible progress and relative stability. Education expanded and became available to many Ecuadorians who previously had no access. In fact, expenditure in education increased 330% from the turn of the century through the final year of Alfaro's presidency, and continued to grow thereafter (see table 3). The state oversaw the construction of communications networks through telegraph lines, roads, and railroads. Urban life was enhanced through the construction of electric lighting and a modernization of postal services, as well as sanitation systems in the biggest cities, of which most famous was that of Guayaquil.

[22] Eloy Alfaro is known as *el viejo luchador* (The eternal fighter) as he had been trying to carry the *liberal revolution* since the first presidency of Gabriel Garcia Moreno (1861-1865).

Table 3: Education Expenditure 1901-1927[23]

Year	Amount (in sucres)	Year	Amount (in sucres)
1899	438,848	1914	1,730,809
1900	524,865	1915	1,401,670
1901	841,403	1916	1,944,016
1902	906,796	1917	1,854,284
1903	872,792	1918	2,510,461
1904	959,956	1919	2,858,065
1905	957,764	1920	3,615,812
1907	1,050,962	1921	3,672,644
1908	1,285,201	1922	3,830,302
1909	1,501,434	1923	3,129,071
1910	1,507,106	1924	3,588,914
1911	1,885,356	1925	3,089,210
1912	1,835,592	1926	3,638,904
1913	2,180,013	1927	4,028,065

Like the railroad, the sanitation of Guayaquil was a leading project of the time. The city was the main port servicing Ecuadorian trade, and if ships anchoring there got contaminated with yellow fever, malaria, plague, or any other of the deadly diseases present at the time, then the port in Guayaquil would have had to be quarantined and no ships would have been able to transport products through its shores. As the U.S. minister to Ecuador told president Plaza in 1912, "the United States might, on occasion, be compelled, however reluctantly, to exclude from passage through the [Panama] canal vessels touching at ports infected with contagious diseases."[24]

The construction of the sanitation system in Guayaquil started after rebels servicing Colonel Carlos Concha Torres, an Alfaro faithful who spearheaded a civil war in 1912,[25] threatened to seize the assets of the U.S. controlled railway. This action provoked the railroad company to plead to the United States' State Department to send help to safeguard their assets. When the United States sent the *Yorktown*, a warship led by Commander

---

[23] Rodriguez, *Government Finances and the Search for Public Policy*, 90. Ecuadorian Ministerio de Hacienda.

[24] Pineo, *Useful Strangers*, 1094.

[25] Officially, colonel Concha Torres started the revolution in the province of Esmeraldas on September 24, 1913.

L. C. Bertolette, the ship contracted yellow fever and three sailors died, including Bertolette. The deaths of these officers and the constant requests by U.S. officials for warships to Ecuadorian waters secured U.S. interest in the sanitation of Guayaquil, which in turn originated the process of its construction.

In 1912, United States' Colonel William Gorgas arrived to conduct a feasibility study for the completion of the sanitation project. President Plaza had agreed with U.S. officials for them to handle development with the exception of all public works, potable water, paving, and sewers, which were to be handled by the British firm J. G. White. As with the railroad, the construction of this project began with difficulty. Ecuador financed the project the same way it had financed the railroad, by pledging the tax revenues collected at the Guayaquil customs house, the same funds that had already been designated for paying railway debt,[26] revenue linked to the cacao trade. Eventually the efforts to clean up the city brought success when the J. G. White Company completed their contract in 1918. And in 1919 the International Health Board of the Rockefeller Foundation launched a program to rid the city of yellow fever, which proved successful when Guayaquil became the last city in South America to eradicate the disease.[27]

War and Leverage of the Ecuadorian Economy

The first decade of the 20th-century came and went smoothly with ousted President Garcia in 1906 being the exception. But then war struck, and before the First World War would menace the world, Ecuador had to deal with the threat of Peru and internal civil war that would be spearheaded by the *Alfaristas*.[28] By August 1911, president Alfaro had been ruling the country for a total of 11 years, 6 with his first tenure, and 5 with his second, and there was discontent.

Since his first days in power Alfaro had ruled with the dogma: *lo Ganado con bayoneta no se puede perder con la papeleta* (what has been

---

[26] Ecuador, during the liberal era, had an international reputation for fiscal irresponsibility. Pledging income that was already allocated to certain projects and creditors, towards other projects and creditors was done more than once.

[27] Pineo, *Useful Strangers*, 1098.

[28] Eloy Alfaro loyals.

won with the bayonets cannot be lost by the ballot). This authoritarian style of maintaining power steadily grew uneasy with the Ecuadorian people. In 1907, Alfaro obtained a majority in congress by registering soldiers three, four, five times so that their vote would be more than that of other citizens.[29] In point of fact, soldiers were registered to vote as many times as needed in as many electoral parishes as demanded so that their number would surpass that of ordinary citizens.[30]

The peoples' reaction was mutiny. The angry crowds gathered outside the presidential palace in Quito demanding fair elections, but were quickly dispersed when soldiers opened fire.[31] This confrontation resulted in several casualties, which have never been completely accounted for as the government purportedly buried the bodies in secret locations out of fear of another rebellion. Nevertheless, a second rebellion would ensue on July of that same year in the city of Guayaquil. This time, the assassination of the president was planned but failed. In retaliation, Alfaro executed the conspirators and dispelled the remaining opposition.[32]

By 1910, however, the uprisings of three years prior seemed forgotten and Ecuador had to deal with its recurrently-bellicose southern neighbor,[33] which if not for the intervention of friendly nations, the two countries would surely have fought a war that year. Consequently, Alfaro was able to unite the country with the help of abundant military

---

[29]Fernando Dobronski, *El Ecuador: Los hechos más importantes de su historia.* (Quito: Soboc Grafic, 2003), 268.

[30] Allegedly, the Liberal era was plagued by continuous electoral frauds. To illustrate: President Antonio Flores Jijón won the election in 1888 with 29,555 votes; Luis Cordero Crespo with 36,557 in 1892; Leonidas Plaza with 62,374 in 1901; Alfredo Baquerizo Moreno with 127,303 in 1916; José Luis Tamayo with 126,945 in 1920; Gonzalo Córdova with 173,773 in 1924; Juan de Dios Martinez Mera with 56,872 in 1932; José María Velasco Ibarra with 51,246 votes in 1934. Academia Nacional De Historia Militar, comp. *Historia militar del Ecuador.* Edited by David Andrade. 1st ed. (Quito: Ministerio de Defensa Nacional del Ecuador, 2010), 412.

[31] These soldiers were led by a foreign commander by the name of Sminger.

[32] Dobronski, *El Ecuador: Los hechos más importantes de su historia,* 268.

[33] Ecuador and Peru had continuous altercations from independence up until the peace treaty signed in 1998.

spending,[34] which had risen 62.83% from the previous year (see table 4), and with a patriotic speech that accompanied his resolute military character as General. At the threat of war with Peru, he decided to lead the Ecuadorian army into battle himself.[35] In essence, Alfaro was able to keep a hold on power by capitalizing on a sentiment of nationalism and through the unhindered expenditure of a growing government treasury driven by revenue from cacao exports (see table 5). Not long afterwards the time came for elections. Alfaro had designated liberal faithful Emilio Estrada to succeed him but found unrelenting opposition to himself and his government and was forced to resign his own presidency only days before his term was to end. After stepping down, Alfaro exiled himself to Panama.

Table 4: Military Expenditure 1895-1927[36]

Year	Amount	Year	Amount
1898	2,629,099	1914	7,599,823
1900	2,048,125	1915	6,593,320
1901	3,413,440	1916	5,112,062
1902	2,384,723	1917	4,764,067
1903	2,496,501	1918	5,861,940
1904	2,354,758	1919	4,568,245
1905	2,293,626	1920	5,343,206
1907	4,043,923	1921	5,501,804
1908	3,276,624	1922	5,892,007
1909	3,614,416	1923	6,214,767
1910	5,885,432	1924	6,709,679
1911	3,585,531	1925	8,132,284
1912	3,758,178	1926	9,230,501
1913	3,933,521	1927	10,143,578

[34] In 1910 Ecuador spent 5,885,432 sucres (See table 6) on the military, a 62.83% increase from the previous year, significantly increasing government expenditure in 1910 (see table 5).

[35] He famously proclaimed: *"Os prometo que si llega el caso, conduciré nuestro ejército a la victoria, siguiendo la sombra egregia de Sucre y obedeciendo los mandatos ultraterrenos del Libertador"* (I promise that if it happens, I will lead our army to victory, following the egregious shadow of Sucre and obeying the unearthly mandates of the Libertador).

[36] Rodriguez, *Government Finances and the Search for Public Policy*, 89.

Table 5: Government Income and Expenditure, 1900-1925[37]

Year	Income (1000s of sucres)	Expenditure (1000s sucres)	Year	Income (1000s sucres)	Expenditure (1000s sucres)
1900	8137	7735	1913	19,845	21,665
1901	10,703	N/A	1914	16,914	20,221
1902	9281	9343	1915	14,885	18,995
1903	10,059	7819	1916	16,053	15,907
1904	8559	10,526	1917	16,572	16,545
1905	11,538	10.156	1918	13,826	17,666
1906	12,922	N/A	1919	15,178	20,046
1907	12,571	12,219	1920	17,214	20,357
1908	12,807	12,675	1921	15,654	21,450
1909	15,895	15,564	1922	18,677	26,568
1910	13,454	25,810	1923	18,532	29,376
1911	13,536	22,437	1924	21,132	35,002
1912	19,973	20,614	1925	36,816	43,890

After a 20-day government in which the president of the Ecuadorian senate would act as head of state, Estrada would assume power on September 1, 1911, but died in office of heart failure only four months into his presidency. The Alfaristas saw this as an opportunity to take power once again and would act accordingly, even though Eloy Alfaro had said that he was returning to the fatherland as a mediator and peacemaker. Leonidas Plaza, who had briefly been minister of finance under Estrada objected, and was consequently drawn into combat by Alfaro's loyal army, which included General Pedro Montero and Flavio Alfaro, Eloy's nephew and new chief of the Alfaristas.[38] Disobeying a key order from his uncle to retreat, Flavio encountered Plaza's and fellow commander Julio Andrade's armies and was forced to capitulate after having been injured and abandoned by fellow Alfarista, General Montero.

After nine days of fighting and three lost battles,[39] the *Flavistas,* which was the term used after Flavio Alfaro took over as leader of the Alfarista

---

[37] Henderson, "Cocoa, Finance and the State in Ecuador," 179.

[38] Flavio Alfaro wanted the Ecuadorian presidency, and presumably he would have become president if the Alfaristas had been victorious in the 1912 conflict against Plaza.

[39] The battles: Defeat at Huigra on January 11, defeat at Naranjito on January 14, defeat at Yaguachi on January 18.

forces, signed a surrender agreement. Not long afterwards, Alfaro and his collaborators were scrambled out of Guayaquil where rampant riots had erupted after Montero was seized by an angry crowd and murdered following his trial and conviction for crimes related to his uprising. On January 28, 1912, they arrived in Quito by the railroad Alfaro had fought so unrelentingly to build, and not hours after they had entered their jail cells, a fuming mob broke into the prison and murdered them. The mad crowd then mutilated their bodies, dragged them through the streets of Quito and burned them at the stake in a public park.[40]

Following the barbaric acts, and after two acting presidents, Leonidas Plaza was once again elected and assumed his post as president for the second time on September 1, 1912. His vision for peace and stability was quickly ended, however, when a year into his administration, an Alfaro faithful, Colonel Carlos Concha Torres, started a revolt in the northwestern province of Esmeraldas. Not long after, 9 months following Colonel's Torres uprising in Ecuador, halfway across the world, the Archduke Franz Ferdinand of Austria was murdered in Sarajevo by a Serbian nationalist[41] and triggered the beginning of the First World War. Consequently on July 28, 1914, exactly one month after the death of the Archduke, the Austria-Hungarian Empire invaded Serbia and officially signaled the start of the war.

Although far from the fighting in Europe, Ecuador would soon feel the effects of the conflict. The belligerence had affected the cacao trade because European nations had interrupted their regular importations due to decreased demand and scarce shipping; as now, naturally, all energies were directed towards the war effort. Before 1914, the accumulative habits in Europe were the necessary ingredient that provided balance to that continent, as large parts of the European surplus capital were invested in the American continent. This enabled Europe to stake out a claim in the natural wealth across the Atlantic.[42] Cacao was not the

---

[40] This infamous incident in Ecuadorian history is known as *La Hoguera Bárbara* (The barbaric bonfire).

[41] Gavrilo Princip was a Bosnian Serb Yugoslavist responsible for the deaths of the Archduke Franz Ferdinand of Austria and his wife, the Duchess of Hohenberg.

[42] At the beginning of the 20th-century, Europe was unable to feed itself and thus the population secured itself through the uninterrupted importation of food and raw materials.

exception, so when this practice was interrupted the Ecuadorian economy began to suffer. During the liberal era, the nation's governments originated between 53% and 81% of their ordinary revenue from customs duties.[43] In 1914, when the First World War broke out, revenue collection was 19% below budget projections; the following year, projections were 29% less than expected.

It was not unfortunate then that the United States was able to leverage Ecuador's trade given the shrinking market for Ecuadorian exports in Europe. The war disrupted the normal patterns of international commerce, and the United States took duty of the import-export trade with Latin America. The European nations that had controlled trade with Ecuador all took minor roles during the war and after. No longer were Ecuadorian products (especially cacao) traded with Britain, France, Germany, and Spain; they were now being offloaded in New York. In 1911, the United States purchased 25% of Ecuadorian exports, but by 1917 the United States was importing 78% of Ecuadorian production. Similarly, in 1911 the United States supplied 27% of all Ecuadorian imports, but by 1917 it would supply 59%.[44] By the 1920s, in the docks of Guayaquil one could no longer see the ships from the British Pacific Steam Navigation Company that had been so common before World War One. In their place, people in the coastal city's port could now observe the growing number of ships from New York's Ward Line Steamship Company.[45]

It was also during the war years that the coastal banking industry, led by the *Banco del Ecuador* and the *Banco Comercial y Agrícola*, would start assuming their pivotal role at the center stage of Ecuadorian finances. Beginning in 1914, internal public debt would grow every year and the banks would obtain an increasing percentage as government's creditors (see table 6). Budget deficits were the norm during the liberal era in Ecuador, regardless of the increased revenue that was being collected at the customs houses. During this time, the active state experienced unprecedented growth, fact that contributed to the ubiquitous deficits.

---

[43] Rodriguez, *Government Finances and the Search for Public Policy*, 104.

[44] Though the United States indeed took over of Ecuadorian trade during WWI, it imposed higher taxes on Ecuadorian products than what the country had been accustomed to while trading with Europe.

[45] Pineo, *Useful Strangers*, 771.

Table 6: Internal public debt in sucres, 1903-1925.[46]

Year[47]	Amount	Percentage owed to Banks
1903	7,060,154	59.8
1909	12,418,845	42.4
1910	13,060,509	51.7
1911	12,570,238	55.2
1912	12,579,838	61.8
1913	14,221,778	57.1
1914	15,229,459	65.9
1915	17,127,497	65.1
1916	18,658,988	64.7
1917	18,827,826	66.8
1918	20,720,518	59.9
1919	22,624,481	66.9
1920	25,647,345	60.4
1921	28,521,573	61.3
1922	32,572,972	63.4
1923	36,032,920	48.6
1924	39,834,542	46.5
1925	49,353,427	67.6

The government's failure to generate balanced budgets forced it to resort to internal bank loans (see tables 7 & 8), which increased persistently due to the unexpected misfortunes of the waning cacao trade and war, which signified astronomical military expenditures that had not been budgeted[48] (see table 4). Furthermore, large amounts of government revenue were allocated by decree, which meant the central government had little room for financial maneuver. The only way the government

---

46 Rodriguez, *Government Finances and the Search for Public Policy,* 116.

47 The years 1903, 1909, 1911,1918, 1923, 1924, 1925 includes government debt only to Banco Comercial y Agrícola and Banco del Ecuador.

48 Since the conflict with Peru in 1910, military expenditures would constantly exceed amounts budgeted.

could manage was by financially operating with the coastal banks. In 1915, the declining cacao revenue resulted in the *Banco Comercial y Agrícola* becoming the principal government lender as the central government scrambled to secure financing.

Table 7: Government debt to Banco del Ecuador in sucres, 1900-1925.[49]

Year	Amount	Year	Amount
1900	1,142,433	1914	3,122,914
1902	1,867,432	1915	3,300,051
1903	2,663,942	1916	3,548,124
1904	2,787,274	1917	3,752,528
1905	2,918,812	1918	4,015,205
1906	2,951,042	1919	4,296,269
1908	2,896,904	1920	4,597,008
1909	2,714,258	1921	4,924,430
1910	2,799,110	1922	5,849,341
1911	2,724,598	1923	5,596,800
1912	3,059,197	1924	5,825,514
1913	3,023,197	1925	6,095,609

Table 8: Government debt to Banco Comercial y Agrícola in scures, 1901-1925.[50]

Year	Amount	Year	Amount
1901	1,332,273	1914	6,706,684
1902	1,622,879	1915	6,715,409
1903	1,556,301	1916	7,251,897
1904	1,430,119	1917	7,712,852
1905	1,287,981	1918	8,402,276
1906	2,362,390	1919	9,390,547
1908	2,519,708	1920	9,936,868
1909	2,547,293	1921	10,334,813
1910	2,471,635	1922	11,218,259
1911	3,586,274	1923	11,909,612
1912	3,825,497	1924	12,678,304
1913	4,907,039	1925	27,262,496

49 Rodriguez, *Government Finances and the Search for Public Policy*, 114.

50 Rodriguez, *Government Finances and the Search for Public Policy*, 115.

Like this, Ecuador withstood the start of World War I with relative ease. However, Ecuadorian cacao growers still found themselves concerned with the global situation of increasing competition in the cacao market, and consequently formed the *Asociación de Agricultores*[51] in 1912 to change the worldwide marketing for their prime asset. The Asociación, which actually received permission and support from the central government to function, aimed to control the price of cacao on the world market.[52] The manner by which they would conduct this was by using the revenue collected through a 1% (eventually 3% in 1916) government allowed tax on cacao exports to purchase national output when prices declined and store it for future sale. The Asociación bought cacao from producers by paying them through a combination of cash and IOUs (*I owe yous*).[53] It then would speculate on price increases. Through this mechanism, the Asociación was purchasing 77% of Ecuador's cacao by 1916.[54]

However, this effort proved fruitless even though in 1916 Ecuador would yield the largest cacao harvest in its history. The following year, the country would lose its dominance due to increased cacao production in Brazil and in the Gold Coast (modern-day Ghana), who would dethrone Ecuador as the world's leading exporter of cacao. In market share, Ecuador lost control of over half the world's production of cacao that it had controlled during the 19th century, to only 14.7% in 1914 and to less than 11% by the start of the 1920s (see table 9). Moreover, plant diseases like Monila Pod Rot in 1917 and the Witches' Broom in 1922, a civil war that would not end until 1916, shortage of shipping (which resulted in soaring freight rates), and world over-production (see table 10) due mostly to African output, which resulted in the tumbling of prices, 78.5% in 15 months (see table 11); all would contribute a fatal blow to the Ecuadorian cacao-export economy. Furthermore, the Asociación's efforts to create a price floor for Ecuadorian export prices aggravated the crisis further after

---

[51] The Farmer's Association.

[52] Similar attempts to control export prices were made at various times elsewhere in Latin America. Brazil succeeded through valorization schemes in the early 20th-century with the help of the federal government. In Chile, nitrate combinations maintained prices between 1884 and 1909. Henderson, "Cocoa, Finance and the State in Ecuador," 180.

[53] Referred to as *Vales* in Ecuador.

[54] Henderson, "Cocoa, Finance and the State in Ecuador," 180.

trying to act as a commodity broker who exported cacao on consignment.[55]

Table 9: Ecuadorian cacao production as a percentage of world production,
1895-1925.[56]

Year	Percentage	Year	Percentage
1895	24.9	1912	14.4
1896	23.9	1913	15.4
1897	21.9	1914	15.3
1898	24.8	1915	11.1
1899	27.7	1916	14.7
1900	18.4	1920	11.7
1901	21.6	1921	10.9
1902	20.1	1922	10.8
1903	18.3	1923	6.7
1904	18.9	1924	6.5
1905-1910	16.2	1925	6.8
1911	15.2		

[55] In 1916, 87% of the cacao controlled by the association was exported on consignment.

[56] Rodriguez, *Government Finances and the Search for Public Policy*, 100.

Table 10: World Cacao Production and Consumption (metric tons) 1895-1925.[57]

Year	World Production	World Consumption
1895	76,212	72,532
1896	72,180	75,868
1897	80,168	83,545
1898	85,174	88,246
1899	99,886	99,376
1900	102,076	100,993
1901	105,820	109,081
1902	123,939	122,185
1903	126,795	127,452
1911	245,043	230,000
1912	232,500	248,800
1913	256,700	254,100
1914	276,900	255,900
1915	296,200	288,900
1916	307,500	260,400
1920	368,385	374,188
1921	380,095	403,180
1922	400,363	421,809
1923	454,270	436,446
1924	499,794	474,212

Table 11: Price of cacao: March, 1920 – June, 1921.[58]

Period	Price per pound
March, 1920	$ 0.2675
December, 1920	$ 0.12
June, 1921	$ 0.0575

[57] Rodriguez, *Government Finances and the Search for Public Policy*, 102.

[58] Rodriguez, *Government Finances and the Search for Public Policy*, 104.

Financial Decline and Revolution

After Plaza completed his second presidency on August 1916, the civil war that had started nearly four years prior in Esmeraldas,[59] would soon end and two stable governments would control Ecuador while it tried to weather out the economic difficulties that were becoming more apparent through every passing year. The Ecuadorian government was able to endure for a few years through the redirection of its trade and with internal loans from coastal banks. Nevertheless, the beginning of a crisis in Ecuador can be pinpointed to the same year as the start of the First World War. In 1914, perhaps out of fear for what eventually would happen, the government added to the list of measures trying to protect the country's livelihood, the *Ley de Inconvertibilidad metálica*,[60] which took the sucre off the gold standard. This law, justified as a means to safeguard the nation's gold reserves, resulted in safeguarding several lending banks, of which the Banco Comercial y Agrícola was the biggest.

News of the war had already ignited financial panic all over the world. Citizens scrambled to protect their wealth by converting their bank notes into gold, and by so doing threatening the stability of financial institutions everywhere. Throughout the globe, nations relaxed or completely abandoned the gold standard. Additional measures like prohibiting gold exports and suspending specie payments were also enacted. In Ecuador, corresponding measures were also taken: gold could not leave the country, government assets backed currency issue, and no currency could be issued while the inconvertibility law was in effect. Also known in Ecuador as the *Ley Moratoria*, the government amended it in 1915 when it became clear that a perpetual prohibition on currency issue was not going to work.

The bill was modified so that banks had the authority to issue currency. This modification demanded that the banks have proper reserves for the money they printed; yet it also allowed them to increase the money supply in proportion to government debt and metallic reserves. This would eventually lead to the devaluation of the sucre as the government continued to finance itself through deficit spending and internal loans. If it were not for the cacao trade, Ecuador would have

---

[59] During the time of this uprising, another uproar led by colonel Carlos Andrade would also materialize, but would be short lived.

[60] Act of metal inconvertibility.

indubitably experienced inflationary problems during the war because the export sector's high productivity meant that the effects of inflation became somewhat diminished. Even after a civil war and the undeniable effects of World War I, as the price and production of cacao remained relatively high, stability lasted until 1925.

In 1917 however, Monilia Pod Rot, one of the most serious diseases affecting cacao in the Americas, ravaged much of the Ecuadorian production. And even though the previous year had been the best in productivity for the country's chief export, things would start to take a turn for the worse. By the start of the following decade the price of cacao was rapidly diminishing along with Ecuador's productivity. In 1920 the price of cacao plummeted from $26 to $6 a quintal,[61] and in 1923, the year after the Witches Broom ravaged plantations all over Ecuador, the country's cacao exports represented a beaten 6.7% of world production. Plantations were ruined. Hacienda Tenguel, which had produced 30,000 quintales of cacao as recently as 1920 was effectively destroyed by 1925 with an output of 883 quintales.[62] In the three years following 1922, the hacienda's workforce was cut in half; no longer were people living in the 300 workers' houses spread over the eight population centers that the property had boasted. As it happened, workers left Tenguel, emigrating to Guayaquil or other nearby haciendas that were beginning to cultivate sugar in response to the collapse of cacao.

The destruction of the nation's topmost export sentenced Ecuador. To balance the diminished revenue from customs duties, the government resorted to uncontrolled borrowing. Foreign lenders were cautious of financing Ecuadorian governments because of the ambivalent attitude they had towards the nation's external debt.[63] The deplorable reputation for honoring debt that Ecuadorians gained was damaged even further when the Asociación de Agricultores was unable to pay the Mercantile Bank of the Americas, which had began representing the Asociación in

---

[61] Pineo, *Useful Strangers*, 1129.

[62] Striffler, *In the Shadows of State and Capital*, 26.

[63] Governments continuously held the belief that Ecuador had never received fair treatment from its creditors and thus took unilateral action to safeguard national interests. Rodriguez, *Government Finances and the Search for Public Policy*, 164.

1916.[64] The dispute for this debt conflict was notorious and lasted for years, a circumstance that spread the dreadful reputation as it also highlighted previous dishonoring of debt.

The Ecuadorian government hence resorted to their longtime financial partners, the coastal banks, for help with the aggravated situation the country was facing. This close relationship between the government and financial institutions in Ecuador existed ever since the banks were created in the 1860s, and was to become ever closer during the first half of the 1920s. From 1920 to 1925, the Ecuadorian government increased internal public debt 92.4%, of which 67.6% was owed to the coastal banks in 1925. Debt to the Banco del Ecuador increased 32.6% from 4,597,008 sucres to 6,095,609 sucres in that half a decade; and debt to the Banco Comercial y Agrícola alone increased from 9,936,868 to 27,262,496 sucres, a monstrous 174.4% increase.

Perhaps even with irresponsible fiscal policy, the cacao bonanza should have shielded the state from having to resort to the banks, even when its production plummeted in the 1920s. It was not that the state did not have access to money; in fact, tax collection and income increased during the liberal era. A significant problem was that with the new money, came uncoordinated laws that directly allocated the newly acquired funds. Congress was averse to establishing criteria for determining necessity and feasibility of new projects, effectively rubber-stamping most of them.

This situation proved disastrous for national finances, and in turn eliminated the ability of government to strengthen its position and avert nationwide instability. Such was the disorganization of new government income that the central government had to resort to the private banks to meet its difficulties. In fact, the local banks eventually financed several of the nation's projects, including the Ecuadorian railroad during the administration of Leonidas Plaza because there was no other way to meet the twice-a-year payments of the foreign-held railway bonds. Apparently, customhouse revenues were not sufficient.

---

64 World over-production, which belittled the demand and value of cacao, resulted in unsold stockpiles of Asociación de Agricultores cacao to build up in Guayaquil and New York. Rodriguez, *Government Finances and the Search for Public Policy,* 110.

The Ecuadorian government in 1900 had absolutely no authority of over 59.5% of ordinary government revenue. On top of this, 65% of the 40.5% the government actually had control of went to the military; hence the government only had 1.9% of ordinary government revenue at its discretion.[65] With these figures, it makes sense that the presidents resorted to banks for aid in financing their administrations as this disorganization of finances continued throughout the liberal era. Therefore, when the crisis heightened in the 1920s, Ecuador let the loans pile up.

Increasing debt, as should have been expected, created chaos in the Ecuadorian economy. Congress had avoided tax reform for decades, so when congress appointed a legislative commission in 1921 to study the national economic and fiscal situation, it was too little too late. The sucre began to devalue, the exchange rate rose from 2.11 sucres per dollar in 1920, to 4.70 sucres per dollar in 1925, a 122.75% increase (see table 12). The decline in value of the sucre during these years more than doubled the cost of importations, which also signified a decline in actual imports that decreased customs revenues. The ever-decreasing revenues and the ever-increasing government expenditures certified that Ecuador would turn head on into a financial abyss.

Table 12: Open market exchange rate of the sucre per dollar, 1920-1926.[66]

Year	Average Rate	Range
1920	2.25	2.11 – 2.60
1921	3.45	2.70 – 3.90
1922	4.20	3.73 – 4.80
1923	4.80	3.60 – 5.80
1924	5.05	4.14 – 5.60
1925	4.35	4.10 – 4.70
1926	4.45	4.45 – 5.56

The depreciation of the sucre, increasing government deficits, and decreased productivity, provoked a serious inflation problem affecting imports and local products. The cost of living in Ecuador increased 27%

---

[65] Rodriguez, *Government Finances and the Search for Public Policy*, 94.

[66] Rodriguez, *Government Finances and the Search for Public Policy*, 97.

from 1920 to 1925,[67] and newspapers would not forfeit the opportunity to report on the cost of food and other necessities. During this time, the press was steered by Luis Napoleón Dillón, a former Plaza minister who had taken the role of chief critic.[68] The unfavorable picture of the state of the country that was being portrayed by the press intensified the already extensive discontent among the Ecuadorian people, and on November, 1922 a general strike and widespread riots paralyzed Guayaquil as workers demanded, among other things, banking law reform as the *tiranía bancaria*[69] was being held responsible for the nation's misfortunes.

The government, wary of accepting demands that would hurt its most essential partners, ignored the demonstrators' petitions, which consequently intensified protests. On the 15th of November the streets of Guayaquil were in chaos, the American Consul General to the city described the strike as "the worst socialistic upheaval that has ever occurred in Ecuador."[70] The protest, fueled by the increasing hardships workers had been enduring, resulted in 89 deaths and 174 wounded people[71] as the manifestations were brought to a brutal end by army troops who opened fire at the crowds.

The massacre of November 1922[72] left a bitter taste in the mouths of all Ecuadorians. Combined with the increasing financial difficulties of the central government and all Ecuadorians in general, the situation was destined to take a drastic turn. In 1924, Ecuador would have the worst production of cacao in its history (39% below 1916 figures) with just 6.5% of world production, which meant the economy lost its main force and the government its key source of revenue. The government's attempts to stabilize exchange rates did not succeed, and only resulted in convincing the Ecuadorian public that the decline in value of their currency was the result of speculation (they did not recognize that the sucre was suffering

---

67 Rodriguez, *Government Finances and the Search for Public Policy,* 98.

68 Luis Napoleon Dillon transpired as lead critic after he failed to be appointed president Gonzalo Cordova's finance minister in 1924.

69 Bankers' tyranny.

70 Henderson, "Cocoa, Finance and the State in Ecuador," 181.

71 Academia Nacional De Historia Militar, comp., *Historia militar del Ecuador,* 413.

72 This incident is the subject of Ecuadorian author Joaquín Gallegos Lara's novel *Las Cruces Sobre el Agua.*

from deficit spending, declining productivity, and world market conditions).

The situation was not good and government opponents from the Ecuadorian sierra used the country's financial upheaval to instill pressure. Luis Napoleon Dillón, who in 1924 vainly aimed at becoming newly elected president Gonzalo Córdova's (1924-1925) finance minister, directed the attack incessantly. It was argued that the outrageous debts by the government to the banks of Guayaquil, and the inaction of Ecuador to return to the gold standard, were part of a successful conspiracy by coastal bankers, especially by the Banco Comercial y Agrícola's general manager Francisco Urbina Jado, to dominate Ecuadorian politics.[73] Growing frustration among Ecuadorian citizens ensured little was done to contradict this propagandistic assessment, and again ignored the facts of what was truly slaying Ecuadorian finances.

Eventually, the situation in Ecuador reached chaotic proportions. Citizens were raucous and the press too. Two newspapers, *La Antorcha*, a Quito socialist publication, and *El Abanderado* a military-oriented one, took their reporting to a whole other level. Their criticism of the coastal banks paved the way for an outright call for rebellion. El Abanderado insisted that young army officers abandon old politics and their superiors, as they had been responsible for the corruption plaguing the country. Further, both newspapers went as far as saying that the Banco Comercial y Agrícola wanted to sell the Galápagos Islands, and that coastal businessmen were actually freemasons loyal to the Grand Lodge in Lima acting on the behalf of Peru, Ecuador's eternal enemy.

And so, in 1924 the campaign launched to convince the young officers that they were the only ones who could save the country from its calamity, proved fruitful. The exhortations of Dillon and his crowd convinced the officers to make a move towards mutiny. As it happened, the country was in financial ruin, increasing the public debt by every passing month, so when president Córdova became ill and traveled to Guayaquil to recuperate, the officers became suspicious that the president was going

---

[73] Luis Napoleon Dillon had a personal quarrel with Urbina Jado because in 1922 Dillon organized the Sociedad de Crédito Internacional de Quito, which intended to issue currency in the sierra region. Noticing that currency from this institution did not have the proper backing, Urbina let the finance minister at the time know of the matter and subsequently currency from Dillon's institution was prohibited from circulating.

there to plan something with the bankers. Thus, on October of that year, a group of lieutenants formed the *Liga Militar* in Quito with the purpose of "saving the country." With the consultation of Luis Napoleon Dillón, the Liga Militar drafted a statement of purpose; it began with the following:

> The great social movements, especially when their purpose is more than economic interests of crude and rude personal positivism should be studied by the redeeming youth of the people; it is up to them, because it is mind and muscle, to be the progenitor of the giant actions that, crystalizing the most beautiful ideas, end in success.[74]

Following the creation of the military league of young officers, the Córdova government attempted to survive, but nine months later any government effort could not avert what would happen; a revolution had begun. The conspiracy by the young officers culminated on July 9, 1925 in what is widely known in Ecuador as the *Revolución Juliana.*[75] The officers, sincere in their ideals, justified their actions in a twelve-point reform program proofread by none other than Luis Napoleon Dillon as he had earned a reputation among the officers as the leading economic and financial expert in Ecuador. Subsequently, he would be named to the provisional government that ran the country after the coup d'état.

The nation had thus entered into the second quarter of the 20th-century in financial ruin and in revolution. The provisional government cultivated the public sentiment and blamed the *tiranía bancaria* for the tragedy, subsequently issuing the arrest of Francisco Urbina Jado, who would die in exile the following year. The revolution, nevertheless, was seen as a beginning of hope for the Ecuadorian people, who trusted that a profound change and better times would come their way. In truth, however, the revolution was the result of regional prejudices and economic misunderstandings, but above all, it was the result of a financial debacle brought about by the decline and fall of the cacao trade, fiscal disorganization and war.

---

[74] Academia Nacional De Historia Militar, comp., *Historia militar del Ecuador,* 416.

[75] Julian Revolution, named after the month on which it took place.

Picture 1: Jose Eloy Alfaro Delgado, head of the Ecuadorian government from 1895 to 1901, and from 1906 to 1911.

Picture 2: Leonidas Plaza, president of Ecuador from 1901 to 1905, and from 1912 to 1916.

Picture 3: Personnel of the Ecuadorian railroad in 1908.

Picture 4: Banco Comercial y Agrícola building during the early 20th century.

Picture 5: Eloy Alfaro riding the Quito-Guayaquil railroad.

Picture 6: Clearing a landslide on the Quito-Guayaquil railway.

Picture 7: Alfaro Loyalists.

Picture 8: Fluvial network.

Picture 9: Preparing cacao for shipment.

Picture 10: Inauguration of the Guayaqui–Quito Railway.

Seated left to right: Archer Harman and Eloy Alfaro. Standing from right to left: Minister Amalio Puga, William H. Fox, General Francisco Hipolito Moncayo, Ministers Cesar Borja, Belisario V. Torres and Alfredo Monje.

Chapter 2
The Age of Crises (1925-1948)

The Julian Revolution on July 9, 1925, put an end to the liberal era that had ruled Ecuador for 30 years. The *tiranía bancaria* was blamed for the misfortunes of the country, but even with all the efforts directed towards disassembling the banking elite, the true reasons for the financial catastrophe that were afflicting the nation could not be ignored. The liberal revolution had failed to bring a progressive transformation to Ecuador. Even with all the infrastructure projects in which the nation's money was spent, a real solution to the country's core problems was nonexistent. The completely inadequate system of public finances, and the inability to free the country from the export sector as the only significant generator of wealth in the economy ended the liberal rule in Ecuador with an out-and-out crisis.

Ecuador would succumb into a period of dreadful events, a disastrous handling of finances, and with cacao absent as a significant financial propeller, instability and suffering is what awaited Ecuadorians. During this time, the changeover of heads of state was a common occurrence, with many of the men leading the country lasting merely months in power. Not even the clamored and respected Kemmerer mission, intent on organizing the nation's finances, was able to survive this chaotic period in Ecuadorian history. Internal instability notwithstanding, in 1941 the country would find itself amid a severe quarrel with Peru. Not being able to organize a proper diplomatic team, and worse, unable to fund a proper military, the Ecuadorian nation would face perhaps the harshest blow in its history.

The years following the overthrow of President Córdova in 1925 initiated a period of change. The "corrupt coastal oligarchy," as the new leaders proclaimed, could no longer enjoy their profits at the expense of the Ecuadorian people; the bankers could no longer hold at their discretion the country's money supply. At the core of the reforms that were to be enacted was the creation of a central bank that would end old regionalist politics and initiate Ecuador's path towards modernization. Consequently, the new regime invited a celebrated team of North American advisers led by Edwin Walter Kemmerer to study the

Ecuadorian situation and suggest the reforms needed to modernize Ecuadorian finances.

Also known as the "Money Doctor," Kemmerer advised countries all over the world. Most famously, he was pursued to help with the financial stabilization of Poland after the First World War, which was in need of new loans, and burdened with a host of unresolved issues. Also on his résumé were missions in Egypt, Germany, India, Mexico, Puerto Rico, and South Africa, among others. Most important for Ecuador, however, were those of Chile, Colombia, and Guatemala, which were considered the blueprint of what needed to be done in the country. The Money Doctor would arrive in Ecuador with the purpose of his mission clear, and his suggestions would become the cornerstone of Ecuadorian reform that would steer the country into the direction it would take the following years.

The Kemmerer Mission and Institutions.

The Julian Revolution was followed by a period of aftershocks; two provisional governments would take power before a new president would be put in office. This period of post-revolutionary politics quickly ostracized the original form of the most pivotal actor of the revolution, the *Liga Militar.* High-ranking majors, colonels, generals, and prominent politicians, most of them from Quito, quickly replaced the young officers who had spearheaded the revolt. Without the input of military men from all across the country who had helped overthrow president Córdova, the officers from Guayaquil and especially Quito, took over the government in the capital. No representatives from the provinces were present to install the new government, as the officers in charge there did not wait for their comrades from the provinces to arrive.

Like this, a Supreme Military Junta consisting of six officers named a Provisional Governing Committee made up of two generals and two civilians from Quito, one of which was Luis Napoleon Dillon. This committee sparked a resounding protest among the representatives from Guayaquil, principally because of Dillon's known fanatical animosity towards the bankers in the coastal city. Nevertheless, the protest did not do much to change the make-up of the new government, the Guayaquil representatives were given "lesser" appointments such as education and social welfare while Dillon's pack were in charge of the ministries of Interior, Foreign Affairs, War and Finance, which was headed by Dillon himself.

Like this, the first *Junta de Gobierno Provisional*, began ruling Ecuador on July 10, 1925. Considering the nature of the propaganda that preceded the coup, the new government decided to issue the arrest of the manager of the largest bank, Francisco Urbina Jado. In point of fact, the first provisional government would become synonymous with causing the demise of the coastal banking system, particularly with actions aimed at destroying Dillon's adversary, Urbina Jado and the Banco Comercial y Agrícola. An investigatory committee established on July 21, 1925, the *Primera Junta Fiscalizadora*, presented its findings concerning the practices of the Ecuadorian banks of issue to Luis Napoleon Dillon on August 22 of the same year. With the consent of the new minister of Finance, the report concluded that Urbina Jado's bank was guilty of circulating un-backed, and thus illegal, currency from 1914 to 1925.

This report, however, seems to have been the result of the post-revolution political warfare that was dictating all aspects of Ecuadorian politics during the time. As it happened, the committee adopted a very questionable definition of what constituted legal reserves and what comprised currency emission. In determining currency reserves, the report ignored the bank's gold holdings abroad, and government assets mortgaged to the bank, hence only considering gold actually deposited at the bank's vault in Guayaquil. The committee also considered all bank notes in circulation as well as all uncirculated bills resting at the bank's vaults. With these interpretations, the commission significantly increased the quantity of what were considered improperly backed bills because the new government considered that legal issues of currency had to be backed up by fifty percent gold reserves held locally. Within these parameters, the bank was guilty as charged. However, it is worth considering that with the inclusion of the bank's holdings abroad, and with the inclusion of government debt as part of its reserves as the legislation drafted in 1914 stipulated, the reserves of the Banco Comercial y Agrícola were always sufficient and frequently bettered the 50% requirement.

To make matters worse, the first provisional government, through Dillon's leadership, created a problematic currency shortage triggered by the increasing political and economic uncertainty that prompted citizens to stockpile legal bills. Plans to create the central bank by transferring undervalued bank reserves, resulted in the banks of issue restricting currency emissions and further fueling the nation's currency problems. Notwithstanding, with the report in hand, which also stated that the bank was solvent, Finance minister Luis Dillon fined the bank 2,237,093.33 sucres[76] and insisted that it be liquidated. Given the significance of the Banco Comercial y Agrícola, Dillon pressed the formation of a Central Bank in order to substitute the institution that had financed the country for over 25 years as both the leading bank of issue and as the government's most important lender. After all, it was the only plausible way that such a bank could be shut down.

The call for change that followed the revolution and Dillon's emphatic fight to liquidate the banking system, set up fitting conditions for the creation of a Central Bank, something Ecuadorians had long considered the establishment of as being of critical importance for the country's modernization. Certainly the coastal bankers themselves, as the actors most concerned with the nation's finances, had been discussing this effort since at least 1920. In point of fact, before the revolution, bankers had urged President Córdova in 1925 to invite Edwin Kemmerer to study the country and offer advice on currency stabilization and the creation of a central bank.[77] Nevertheless, Dillon and the first provisional government, although decided on establishing a central bank in Ecuador, had a different idea on how to go about it. They had no interest in paying a foreign advisor and instead proposed forming the central bank by confiscating the metallic reserves of the country's banks of issue by paying them half the world market value for their gold.[78]

Understandably, the coastal bankers became wary of this proposition that was to be executed by an extra-legal government and that would have destroyed their patrimony. They insisted that no action of this magnitude be enacted until a constitutional government was elected and a commission of experts offered their recommendations. The arguments that ensued quickly degenerated into a political battle between the coastal and sierra regions in which the local newspapers often favored the local viewpoints. The situation of the country was not getting any better and the public had no patience for any bickering. Discontent with the government, and disputes among the members of the Junta, forced the resignation of the provisional government, and appointed a second *Junta*

---

[76] Rodriguez, *Government Finances and the Search for Public Policy*, 128.

[77] The coastal bankers offered to help with the financing of a Kemmerer advisory mission in 1925.

[78] Rodriguez, *Government Finances and the Search for Public Policy*, 129.

de Gobierno Provisional that would govern the country from January 10 through March 31, 1926.

The new government saw Dillon lose his post as finance minister, and new minister Humberto Albornoz would distance himself from the confrontational ways of his predecessor. In order to reach consensus, Albornoz hosted a banker's conference where the country's economic condition was to be discussed and solutions proposed. In this meeting, one of the main concerns was the government's hostility towards the banks, which had intensified the public's lack of confidence in financial institutions. In particular was the attack against the Banco Comercial y Agrícola because the bank issued the vast majority of currency then in circulation. And with the new definitions of reserve requirements, the recall of "illegal" bills, as other banks had done, would have resulted in the inability to conduct transactions, as the already present currency shortage would have worsened.

The solutions that were therefore proposed included the creation of a government office appended to the Ministry of Finance where currency backed by government assets, mortgage bonds, or a reduced metallic reserve could be issued. But mainly, the conference suggested the assistance of a foreign advisory mission to help with the nation's financial problems. The government's reaction was to reject most of the solutions proposed at the bankers' conference; however it did reopen the idea of negotiating with Edwin W. Kemmerer. When the Junta replaced the second provisional government with a single executive on April 1926, the process of bringing Kemmerer was finally concluded when the new head of government, former minister of Welfare, Isidro Ayora (1926-1931), reached an agreement with the Princeton economist.

Before Kemmerer would arrive in Ecuador on October 1926, the post-coup financial crisis got worse. The post-coup governments' actions had aggravated the situation through their policies against financial entities, so it was not long before the government was forced to take additional measures to try to save the country from crumbling further. On June 16, 1926, interim president Ayora[79] ordered the embargo of the metallic reserves of the banks of issue at a value less than half their actual market

---

[79] The final arbiter of Ecuadorian politics at the time, the Supreme Military Junta, opposed a premature return to a constitutional government. Thus Ayora ruled the country as interim president for 3 years.

price;[80] following this, on June 23, he established the *Caja Central de Emisión y Amortización* (Central fund of Issue and Redemption), which was authorized to issue currency with 25% metallic reserves as opposed to the 50% requirement specified for the former banks of issue. The new reserve created under the Caja provided backing for all bills in circulation as well as notes printed not in use.[81] The Caja further consolidated itself by transferring government indebtedness to banks towards the Caja and agreeing to amortize this debt with revenues from export duties.[82]

Four months after the Caja had taken over the Ecuadorian currency, Edwin Walter Kemmerer finally arrived in Guayaquil on the 18th of October 1926. He would find a nation that between August 1923, and July 1925, had expended two constitutional presidents, one acting president, a plural executive, and five ministers of finance, and from then on, a nation that had undergone a revolution that had ended in an authoritarian regime that had already positioned three provisional governments in 14 months. Unsurprisingly, he would also find a country with severe financial problems that included a faded export economy, currency shortage, lack of financial institutions, and the lowest rating for government bonds in all of Latin America.[83]

With a worldwide reputation as a foreign financial advisor, Kemmerer initiated his repute as a specialist in currency reform and central banking in 1903 as a member of the United States Philippines Commission. During his three-year stay in the Philippines, he drafted laws for implementing the agricultural bank of the islands, he placed the currency on the gold standard, and acted as chief of the division on currency. From then on, he would travel to countries all over the world and mimic the practices he had initiated in the Philippines. As Kemmerer historian, Paul Drake, notes, "hardly a word [of his proposals] ... varied from Poland to Bolivia,"[84] thus the coastal bankers and the government understood what

---

80 Rodriguez, *Government Finances and the Search for Public Policy*, 132.

81 Printed un-circulating bills had been included in the government's assessment regarding illegal currency of the issuing banks.

82 This agreement violated the terms accorded with the Guayaquil-Quito Railway bondholders.

83 Pineo, *Useful Strangers*, 1171.

84 Quoted in Pineo, *Useful Strangers*, 1175.

a Kemmerer mission would recommend for Ecuador. Kemmerer, with a cost to the government of $70,000 plus all expenses (equivalent to over $930,000 in 2015), would recommend currency stabilization as well as devaluation, tax reform, a central bank in the capital and the modernization of the banking system as a whole, and naturally, the obligatory placement of the currency on the gold standard.

Once on Ecuadorian soil, the Kemmerer mission was greeted with hope and enthusiasm. The press, who had been divided just a few months back due to the discrepancies between the coastal bankers and the government, was now united in praise towards Kemmerer and his team. It was not uncommon to find newspapers with favorable biographical articles on all the people who integrated the mission. Articles with statistical information and suggestions to the mission were also widely printed in daily newspapers and other periodicals; interested citizens even sent letters with recommendations to the mission. The enthusiasm went as far as producing outright fallacy when newspapers in Quito, with alleged information from sources in New York, asserted that various Wall Street tycoons had decided on lending money to Ecuador and Bolivia because of the sole fact that they had hired the services of Edwin Kemmerer.[85] In truth, nothing could have been further from reality as Ecuador continued to struggle for credit consideration long after the mission left.

The mission followed a strict work schedule from the offices allotted to them in the recently inaugurated post office building in the center of Quito from which the final recommendations were submitted to the government on February and March of 1927.[86] The report consisted of over two thousand pages of proposed laws and reports on specific topics, all attached with the required explanatory statements. It was Kemmerer's practice to deliver drafts of laws ready to present to congress, and drafts of administrative decrees ready to be stamped by the executive as opposed to a single comprehensive report. This enabled the advisors to control the exact wording of the laws, thus eliminating the possibility of vague and confusing edicts that could have gone against his overall idea for the

---

[85] Paul Drake, *Kemmerer en los Andes* (Quito: Banco Central Del Ecuador, 1995), 229.

[86] The mission was unable to complete its work by the established date of February of 1927 because the Ecuadorian government requested the advisors for studies that had not been part of the initial agreement.

country. Although organized and efficient, the advisors were not always very careful. Vast sections of the report were simply borrowed from the work done in other countries. For instance, Robert Vorfeld, the expert in customs administration who had worked with the Tariff Commission in Washington, simply copied the work he had done in Paraguay. This resulted in unnecessary customs regulations to Ecuador's internal waterway traffic because in Paraguay, external commerce was transported through the international river that bears that country's name.[87]

Nonetheless, Ayora and the Ecuadorian people in general were quite pleased with the mission's work. Such was the case—or perhaps it was due to the fact that Colombia had started borrowing money from overseas banks almost immediately after putting its Kemmerer program in place—that the dictatorship expeditiously made into law the entirety of Kemmerer's recommendations. After all, Ecuador's economy was in dire straits and the government needed money quickly. The recommendations, as expected, sought to achieve "exchange stability, modern banking, fiscal order, more efficient customs administration, punctual debt payments, Anglo-Saxon commercial practices, and equal rights for foreign capitalists."[88] These goals were organized into two main objectives categories: the modernization and strengthening of Ecuadorian institutions and procedures, and the elimination of budget deficits. To accomplish the first, a new system for managing public funds and regulating the fiscal and banking systems was proposed. To accomplish the second, it was to be achieved through the centralization of government income, a new tax system, and through the implementation of a national budget over which government funds would be allotted.[89]

With his recommendations, Kemmerer employed a western orthodox economic thought of the time. His reports on tariff reform, contracts, and banking law closely resemble Woodrow Wilson's New Freedom policies in which the United States eased on free trade, severely punished unlawful business practices and initiated the federal reserve system. In point of fact, the mission's tariff reform was frequently criticized for its *laissez-faire* policies that Ecuadorians thought would condemn Ecuador to an agrarian collapse. Kemmerer, as he would always favor, also insisted on the gold

---

[87] Drake, *Kemmerer en los Andes,* 257.

[88] Pineo, *Useful Strangers,* 1184.

[89] Rodriguez, *Government Finances and the Search for Public Policy,* 143.

standard even when Ecuador and many countries in Europe and America suspended convertibility due to the difficulties arising from the First World War. His approach went in accordance with Great Britain's Gold Bullion standard established in 1925 whereby currency was backed by gold, but in which gold would not exist in circulation. Even the focus on government spending in public works practiced by Herbert Hoover and later Franklin Roosevelt was taken into account when addressing Ecuador's public credit and public works development. At the time, the theory of under-consumption, which suggested that strong government spending on public works was necessary to restore the balance between production and consumption, was gaining momentum and Kemmerer seems to have included it within his suggestions.

The reforms thus addressed the problems that were perceived to be incapacitating Ecuador to achieve any sort of financial stability. The public works disorganization—which had been an integral part of the financial debacle that affected Ecuador when the cacao trade imploded, and when between 1914 and 1925 over twenty million dollars were spent with few tangible results—was changed so that those funds be diverted into servicing the country's foreign debt and strengthening public credit. Public works hereafter were to be funded by foreign loans or direct foreign investment, and be analyzed by a central comprehensive national planning program that would forbid Congress' practice of aimlessly appropriating funds for almost any program promoted by sectional interests.

Principal state institutions were created through new laws: the Central Bank of Ecuador, the Superintendence of Banks, the Comptroller General, and the Director General of Customs. Together these institutions brought about profound change in Ecuador, because even though many of the Kemmerer reforms would soon be forgotten, these institutions would continue to exist, and with great power. Immediately after their creation, for example, the Central Bank would place the country under the gold standard and define the discount rate. The superintendence of banks would begin regulating lending entities, and the comptroller General (*La Contraloría*) would begin monitoring government finances. The Director General of customs would, from 1925 to 1930, increase customs revenue from 19% to 25% of all imports,[90] consequently considerably increasing customs revenue for the central government (see table 13).

---

[90] Drake, *Kemmerer en Los Andes*, 257.

Table 13: Customs revenue 1925-1947[91]

Year	Absolute amount (in sucres x 1000)	% of ordinary Government revenue
1925	20,284	55
1926	19,005	42
1927	23,277	36
1928	26,728	43
1929	27,806	43
1930	23,309	38
1931	17,496	39
1932	12,702	30
1933	12,582	30
1934	20,201	42
1935	29,118	44
1936	31,011	40
1937	30,161	34
1938	45,303	37
1939	35,571	30
1940	43,518	40
1941	38,709	36
1942	53,398	41
1943	67,501	40
1944	95,237	45
1945	90,203	36
1946	99,615	33
1947	152,626	39

Furthermore, some of the structural transformations promoted by the Kemmerer mission signified changes of a revolutionary nature because even though many of the propositions included in the 2000 page report were not new, the circumstances surrounding them were. 19 months after the Julian Revolution, Ecuadorians still had the sour memories that surrounded the uproar fresh in their minds. People were ready for change, and the press stimulated this openness through extensive coverage of the mission's reports. Journalists from media outlets throughout the country emphasized that the recommendations were not the product of partisan politics but the work of true independent scientists, and even supported the idea of foreigners directing the newly created institutions and procedures because it was believed no Ecuadorian had the expertise necessary to carry out the required

[91] Rodriguez, *Government Finances and the Search for Public Policy*, 188.

functions properly. Few newspapers remembered the less than desirable experience the nation had with another foreign advisor, John Hord, a few years prior. And so, when the Kemmerer mission departed to Bolivia in mid-March 1927, all but one of the newly appointed American administrators were already working at their posts.

Even when Ecuadorians expected better days after Kemmerer, many still felt the crisis affecting their everyday lives. Many believed regionalist politics would eventually thwart the implementation of the money doctor's reforms, especially if the country returned to constitutional government before they were carried through. Thus, on March 4, 1927, opponents of the Ayora administration attempted to overthrow the president and put General Gomez de la Torre as *Jefe Supremo* in his place. The attempt ended in failure, and Ayora used his position as dictator to quickly charge disgruntled bankers and his perceived adversaries as being responsible for the coup attempt. He then swiftly arrested them before anyone could challenge the accusations. Nevertheless, the propaganda used by the government against the conspirators, responsible or not as they may have been, strengthened the Ayora regime's political position, and attention was once again directed towards Kemmerer and the advice he would leave behind.

Depression

After the Kemmerer mission left Ecuador, the country hoped the reforms, which were immediately enacted almost to their entirety, would attract foreign investors and lines of credit. Unfortunately, even after improving procedures and creating new institutions, the money was not coming. Concerning this matter, Edwin Kemmerer warned the Ecuadorian people that they would need to be steadfast and patient, especially because the continuous default on loan payments across the nation's history had meant that Ecuadorian government bonds possessed a dreadful rating, the lowest in South America. As a matter of fact, at least for 72 out of the 97 years, from 1830 to 1927, the Ecuadorian government had constantly defaulted on loan payments. Further, he signaled that if and when Ecuador gained access to credit, these loans would come with high interest rates, and most probably request customs revenue as collateral.

It was also not helpful that the country had undergone a revolution in 1925 and subsequently produced three unconstitutional governments. Regarding this, the United States refused to recognize any of these extra-legal administrations, and thereby further hampering the Ecuadorian hope for foreign capital. It was not even enough that Kemmerer himself tried to persuade bankers and government officials that Ecuador, having enacted his reforms, was worthy of diplomatic acknowledgement and financial backing. Kemmerer went as far as saying in 1927 to the United States Department of State, that Ecuador, now probably had the most honest government in its history and that the United States should find some way to recognize it as soon as possible.

Kemmerer's insistence was further fueled when he informed the Department of State that, after his conversations with North American leading bankers, diplomatic recognition of Ecuador would reinforce their intentions to grant financing to the country. It had been the bankers' opinion that the management of the customs office satisfied the conditions they were looking for to grant any potential loan because now they could reliably be guaranteed by customs revenue. Yet at the same time, the United States government was receiving pressure from the long-standing and unattended bondholders, whose bonds had been issued during the construction of the Ecuadorian railroad. They insisted no recognition be granted until they were reimbursed. To this, the money doctor pointed out the unsolvable dilemma of the Ecuadorian problem. He exposed the fact that payment to the existing bondholders could not be carried out until the country received financial backing, which was in turn conditioned on the United States government recognizing the Ecuadorian. He further expressed his opinion that any real possibility of bondholders getting their money was not with a Latin American congress, as it would never approve a reasonable liquidation, but with a progressive dictatorship like that of Ayora. So, it was not until August 1928, when an election for a new National Assembly was announced, that the United States finally granted *de jure* recognition to Ecuador.[92]

Nevertheless, given the absence of a legal requisite that would have mandated the United States' Department of State to approve foreign lending, Kemmerer insisted that lenders take Ecuador into consideration. Such was the case, that in early 1928, Kemmerer helped the Ayora government convince the Dillon, Read & Company, as well as other corporations, to facilitate financing. These negotiations produced the visit from former Kemmerer mission general secretary, Edward Freely, to Quito and discuss loan terms with Ecuadorian officials. This visit only produced

---

[92] Drake, *Kemmerer en los Andes*, 259.

negative reactions from both governments. The United States government was furious, not only at the fact that Ecuador was being considered for North American financing when its government wasn't even recognized yet, but also because congress was entertaining the idea of cancelling the North American functionaries' contracts. In Ecuador, the visit was seen as blackmail by the United States government, as it was believed that Ecuador was being pressured into signing a high-interest loan just so that the country could receive diplomatic recognition.

Thus the hopes for foreign capital did not materialize. While the rest of Latin America was offered plenty of money, taking in the 1920s more loans than at any time until the 1970s,[93] Ecuador would have to accept a different situation. In the end, the only foreign loan Ecuador would receive during the 1920's came in the immediate aftermath of the Kemmerer mission when on November 1927, the Swedish Match Company advanced 8 million sucres to the government in exchange for a 25-year monopoly to import and produce matches in Ecuador. The Ecuadorian government would use these resources to fund the *Banco Hipotecario del Ecuador* in 1928 with the aim of helping local farmers.

Ecuador's struggles for financing were accompanied by an effort to restore constitutional rule, which put in place the constitution of 1929 with Isidro Ayora as constitutional president. This *magna carta* attempted to constitute Ecuador within a parliamentary organization. Essentially, this implied that any legislator could individually challenge any minister of state and ask for their denunciation, or request a motion of no confidence. This resulted in the legislative branch turning into a mob-like institution where appointments would be negotiated and imposed on the president. With this constitution, the president was effectively stripped of the powers he was used to having; this being especially true with Isidro Ayora and his three-year dictatorship.

Following the change of country charter, which included the prearrangement that foreign functionaries were no longer permissible, Ecuador would deviate from the procedures that had been put in place by the Kemmerer mission. In point of fact, the departure by Ecuadorian institutions from what the mission had envisioned, was already acknowledged in 1929 by the departing foreign functionaries. As

---

[93] Pineo, *Useful Strangers*, 1189.

Kemmerer mission member Tompkins proclaimed to the Ecuadorian National Assembly that same year:

> While the Kemmerer Mission does not need any defense, however, if judged only by its results, it could be affirmed that its visit to Ecuador was a complete fiasco. It really was, but not because of the mission itself... In light of subsequent events, it is clear that the whole issue of taking the services of the Kemmerer mission and its various consultants was merely a beautiful gesture. One objective was, of course, to influence public opinion within the country. The other objective, and most important, was directed to create favorable propaganda abroad and get a loan.[94]

The deviation from what had been spawned by the Kemmerer mission would become a risky proposition for Ecuador. The first years of the Ayora administration had been accompanied by a favorable export market and by the Kemmerer reforms, which produced favorable financial outcomes. When Kemmerer's recommendations ceased to be followed, spearheaded by the decrease in executive power as a result of the new constitution of 1929, the country was able to maintain relative stability because of the then still-unwavering export market. From 1925 to 1928, Ecuador maintained a favorable trade balance mainly due to the still-relevant cacao trade, which still represented 38.5% and 30.1% of total exports in 1927 and 1928 respectively (see table 14). Also important, was Ecuador's somewhat diversification in export products, nearly every other product increased its percentage rate of total exports with relation to 1925 (see table 15). Consequently, from 1926 to 1929, customs revenue as a percentage of national government income was always over a sustaining 43% (see table 16).[95]

---

[94] Drake, *Kemmerer en los Andes*, 267.

[95] In 1927 government income from currency revaluation caused customs percentage to fall to 36%. However, if government revenue from this source is excluded, customs revenue was 45% of income that year.

Table 14: Cacao exports 1925-1947[96]

Year	Kg x 1000	Value in Sucres x 1000	% of total exports
1925	32,281	33,986	46.7
1926	20,567	26,436	41.6
1927	22,238	36,908	38.5
1928	23,737	29,653	30.1
1929	16,386	21,256	24.7
1930	19,184	23,403	29.0
1931	13,839	12,254	21.6
1932	14,419	11,267	22.9
1933	11,004	8,720	19.7
1934	16,143	27,165	25.0
1935	19,701	23,828	21.0
1936	17,114	31,472	21.6
1937	20,652	49,985	30.5
1938	16,882	39,276	36.6
1939	13,276	37,033	22.1
1940	11,208	29,354	17.5
1941	14,433	34,364	17.2
1942	13,761	40,326	13.5
1943	16,827	51,793	13.2
1944	15,750	41,985	9.0
1945	16,827	53,547	14.2
1946	16,526	74,934	15.8
1947	19,757	189,038	32.8

Table 15: Selected exports by percent value of total exports 1925-1930[97]

Year	Coffee	Rice	Panama Hats	Crude Oil
1925	10.5	0.2	4.4	0.6
1926	18.1	0.5	8.7	3.5
1927	10.0	1.1	6.1	5.6
1928	17.6	2.9	4.6	12.3
1929	13.6	4.9	7.9	17.7
1930	9.4	4.6	10.4	21.4

[96] Rodriguez, *Government Finances and the Search for Public Policy*, 192.

[97] Rodriguez, *Government Finances and the Search for Public Policy*, 180-181.

Table 16: Customs revenue as a percentage of national government income 1925-1947[98]

Year	Absolute Amount x 1000	% of income
1925	20,284	55
1926	19,005	42
1927	23,277	45 (36 with currency revaluation)
1928	26,728	43
1929	27,806	43
1930	23,309	38
1931	17,496	39
1932	12,702	30
1933	12,582	30
1934	20,201	42
1935	29,118	44
1936	31,011	40
1937	30,161	34
1938	45,303	37
1939	35,571	30
1940	43,518	40
1941	38,709	36
1942	53,398	41
1943	67,501	40
1944	95,237	45
1945	90,203	36
1946	99,615	33
1947	152,626	39

Nevertheless, the Ecuadorian economy, and therefore its steadiness as a nation, hung by a thread towards the end of the 1920s. The Wall Street Crash of 1929, perhaps the most devastating stock market crash in the history of the United States, signaled the beginning of the Great Depression in that nation, which affected virtually all Western economic powers and their connected economies. Ecuador, having the North Americans as its most important economic partner, would too feel the effects of the worldwide financial catastrophe in its totality. In 1929, 47% of Ecuador's exports were to the United States; similarly, 41% of all Ecuadorian imports came from the North American nation. After the implosion of cacao, what remained of Ecuador's export economy collapsed. Ecuadorian exports fell by two-thirds from 1928 to 1932, similarly all imports contracted by a factor of 64.7% during the same

---

[98] Rodriguez, *Government Finances and the Search for Public Policy*, 188.

period.[99] Consequently, after 1929 (see table 16), customs revenue as a percentage of national government income receded continuously and government income as a whole suffered as a result (see table 17).

Table 17: National government income 1925-1946[100]

Year	Absolute amount x 1000, in sucres	Year	Absolute amount x 1000, in sucres
1925	36,816	1926	44,856
1927	65,150	1928	61,576
1929	64,480	1930	60,821
1931	45,270	1932	42,162
1933	41,842	1934	48,242
1935	66,486	1936	77,464
1937	86,585	1938	120,833
1939	117,187	1940	108,553
1941	109,001	1942	128,985
1943	168,284	1944	211,958
1945	252,717	1946	298,813

Government income was precipitously diminishing, which resulted in a government budget fiasco. From 1930 to 1938 the government experienced continuous deficits (see table 18), even when bank loans were considered part of government revenue, and even with the revaluation of gold reserves in 1935. This undoubtedly instilled greater pressure on the governments that ruled Ecuador in the 1930s. Ayora was the one who experienced the offset of the worldwide depression, and the problems with the state budget were accompanied by an ever-increasing cost of living for Ecuadorians as most of the products of basic necessity were on a steady cost increment in relation to wages (see table 19). Henceforward, even though large parts of the Ecuadorian population at the time lived in rural areas and therefore could not experience the effects of depression as much as the urban population did, the restlessness of the Ecuadorian people grew.

---

[99] Pineo, *Useful Strangers*, 1206.

[100] Rodriguez, *Government Finances and the Search for Public Policy*, 219.

Table 18: Projected vs actual government income, 1925-1940[101]

Year	Budgeted Income (thousands of sucres)	Actual Income (thousands of sucres)	Surfeit/Deficit
1925	35,833	36,816	983
1926	41,988	44,856	2,868
1927	41,988	75,211	33,223
1928	51,588	74,866	23,278
1929	59,900	64,480	4,580
1930	64,037	60,821	(3,216)
1931	61,476	45,270	(16,206)
1932	49,115	42,162	(6,953)
1933	49,220	41,842	(7,378)
1934	48,970	48,242	(728)
1935	48,970	66,486[102]	17,516
1936	80,100	77,464	(2,636)
1937	79,500	86,585	7,085
1938	120,500	120,833	333
1939	130,950	117,187	(13,763)
1940	113,050	108,533	(4,517

Table 19: Price index for basic necessity goods, 1925-1943[103]

Year	Index	Year	Index
1925	145.4	1926	182.3
1927	169.7	1928	138.9
1929	144.3	1930	143.3
1931	106.4	1932	100.09
1933	134.5	1934	185.6
1935	180.5	1936	220.3
1937	264.1	1938	255.7
1939	256.9	1940	262.4
1941	284.8	1942	370.8
1943	427.6		

Social dissatisfaction began in 1930 with student revolts and a coup attempt led by General Francisco Gómez de la Torre. In the same manner,

---

101 Rodriguez, *Government Finances and the Search for Public Policy*, 229.

102 Includes income from the revaluation of gold reserves.

103 Rodriguez, *Government Finances and the Search for Public Policy*, 171.

indigenous uprisings struck Ecuador in 1931, like those of *Quito Corral* and *Tanilagua*; *Palmira* and *Pastocalle* in 1932; *Mochapata* in 1933; and *Rumipamba*, *Llacta Urco* and *Salinas* in 1934.[104] Discontent was ever-present; the uprising by military sappers from Chimborazo, followed by a mob in Quito who went up in arms demanding undeliverable relief measures, resulted in the forced resignation of President Ayora on August 24, 1931. Pressured by a faction of the military who wanted colonel Luis Larrea Alba in power, Ayora appointed him as secretary of state so that he would, as the constitution established, assume the presidency after his resignation.

Larrea held office for less than two months. He believed that congress had to grant him extraordinary powers so that he could resolve the problems facing the nation. When congress refused, with the consent of the military, he decided to abolish it. This action provoked an enraged outcry by the citizenry, which resulted in the death of 10 people, with other dozens injured.[104] Following this despicable incident, Larrea resigned, and president of the senate and former president of Ecuador, Alfredo Baquerizo Moreno, took office on October 15, 1931. As his first executive order, he convened presidential elections to be held on October 20 and 21. With 48% of the 54,320 votes counted, former president of the Central Bank of Ecuador, Neptalí Bonifaz, was elected president due to overwhelming support in the sierra region (see table 20).

Table 20: Election of 1931[105]

Candidate	Votes	Percent of votes
Neptalí Bonifaz Ascázubi	26,062	48
Modesto Larrea Jijón	15,630	28.8
Ildefonso Mendoza Vera	12,628	23.2
Total	54,320	100.0

The president-elect would never serve. Widespread discontent, which included frequent bungled revolts, exacerbated the nation's problems. The financial devastation was accompanied by a full-swing political and social meltdown. The 1931 election aimed at restoring constitutional government by instating the third government since the resignation of

---

[104] Academia Nacional De Historia Militar, comp., *Historia militar del Ecuador*, 432.

[105] Rodriguez, *Government Finances and the Search for Public Policy*, 165.

Ayora two months prior. However, this would not happen. Ecuador was divided; every section of the country was clashing, liberals and conservatives, serranos and costeños. Worsening things was the fact that the constitution of 1929 stipulated that the final vote count of the elections was to be done by the following legislature meeting, which was to take place on August 1932, a full 10 months away. This left plenty of time for things to take a turn for the worse.

On January 1932, liberal loyalists to Larrea Jijón attacked the military barracks in Tulcán, in northern Ecuador, only to end in failure. Three months later, in April, military commander Mendoza led the Ecuadorian navy into revolt only to be defeated too. The following month, university students took to the streets in protest only to be disbanded by a garrote-armed coalition of *Bonifacistas*[106] and the police. The continuous social and political unrest did not cease to be accompanied by the continuous financial catastrophe. The assurances of government officials and foreign experts that the country would be able to successfully weather out the depression did not convince the Ecuadorian people. They continued to make unattainable demands for relief; they insisted the government introduce tariff measures that would raise agricultural and industrial production. To these demands the government yielded, and in retrospect they committed a terrible mistake in doing so.

The procedures instilled by the Kemmerer mission that had proven fruitful for over a quarter decade had long been abandoned in the 1930s. After President Ayora left office, any hopes of carrying the Kemmerer reforms through were gone. In its place, the Ecuadorian governments experimented with an array of measures that hoped would improve economic conditions. The government attempted to control trade through the implementation of protectionist and preferential tariffs, exchange controls, restrictions on imports, payments in nonconvertible currencies, and special bilateral agreements. Mind-bogglingly, customs revenue was all but eliminated through the placement of additional tariff charges that severely hampered customs transactions. The *aduana*[107] as a source of revenue was abandoned in favor of crackpot protectionist policies.

---

[106] Bonifaz loyals.

[107] Customs house.

As an export economy, it was inconceivable that such actions took place in Ecuador. Authorities even tried to find a niche in the spirits market in the United States. In 1933, the end of prohibition in the northern nation made many Ecuadorians reason that the economy could get a boost by exporting locally produced *aguardiente*.[108] But consumers in the United States had little interest in aguardiente, Ecuadorian or otherwise. Yet perhaps most troubling of all the effects of the doomed government experimentation during the worldwide depression, was the uncertainty among the economically active community. Governments lasted months, while ministers would be replaced within weeks. Policies, tariffs and taxes changed at similar rates. The uncertainty this instability instilled in investors and entrepreneurs effectively killed any possibility of new capital entering the suffering Ecuadorian economy. The government's efforts unequivocally failed and injured rather than aided Ecuador's economic recovery in the 1930s.

With customs revenue falling, diminishing over 30% from 1929 to 1932 with respect to its share of government income (table 16), the government had to resort to the central bank for help. Just as governments had done in the 1920s, governments in the 1930s ran to the banks in order to try and finance their regimes; not much was learned, little had changed. What did change was the fact the in the 1930s, the lender became the Central Bank. This institution's conservative policies could not offset the depletion of the country's gold reserves or the contraction of the money supply. In 1927, the year the bank was founded, Ecuador possessed 44,085,490 sucres in metallic reserves. Within the next few years, however, Ecuador would sell more gold than it purchased every year until the country went off the gold standard in February 1932. The gold drain was so extreme that when inconvertibility went into effect, the nation possessed 17,408,986 sucres in metallic reserves (see table 21), a 60.5% decrease from 1927. By the end of the decade, grams of gold reserves would decrease by 75.3%.

[108] Anise-flavored spirit distilled from sugar cane.

Table 21: Central Bank of Ecuador gold reserves, 1927-1939[109]

Year	Amount in sucres[110]	Grams of Gold
1927	44,085,490	13,266,779
1928	38,029,255	11,449,990
1929	35,063,646	10,557,440
1930	28,639,062	8,618,439
1931	15,492,532	4,662,214
1932	17,408,986	5,088,230
1933	18,340,216	5,327,337
1934	27,156,303	5,846,330
1935	38,830,834	3,862,192
1936	42,525,686	3,643,202
1937	39,890,498	3,386,173
1938	39,798,376	3,216,639
1939	40,857,151	3,271,275

The depleting gold reserves came in conjunction with the contraction of the money supply. In 1931, the monetary circulation was less than half of what it had been in 1927 (see table 22). The effect of this contraction was felt by the Ecuadorian people, and again instilled pressure on the government to take action. The public diagnosis was that the retrenchment of the money supply was the cause, not the result, of the financial crisis. Thus, pressure was put forth on the government to increase currency emission as well as to reclaim funds earmarked for debt service in order to meet domestic needs. If the depleting gold reserves, the contraction of the money supply, and continuous government experimentation with financial policy were not enough, on the same day the gold standard was repealed, the president signed a decree obliging the Central Bank to lend the government fifteen million sucres for public works projects, agricultural credit, and for servicing public debt.

[109] Rodriguez, *Government Finances and the Search for Public Policy*, 168.

[110] Gold reserves were revaluated twice, first on December 18, 1935 when price changed from 3.3229 sucres per gram of gold to 9.968331 sucres; and then on June 13, 1936 when the price of gold was established at 11.6466 sucres per gram.

Table 22: Monetary circulation, 1927-1946[111]

Year	Amount	Year	Amount
1927	38.7	1937	68.1
1928	36.5	1938	73.1
1929	30.0	1939	77.9
1930	23.5	1940	80.2
1931	19.1	1941	120.2
1932	30.3	1942	169.3
1933	43.1	1943	232.2
1934	56.7	1944	294.6
1935	59.9	1945	321.2
1936	67.1	1946	349.7

The decree started a negative borrowing spiral resembling that of the previous decade. Between March 1932 and August 1937, the Ecuadorian government borrowed 47 million sucres from the Central Bank.[111] These funds were mostly used to cover budget deficits, fund public works projects, finance military expenditures, and to pay off the government's debt to the Banco Hipotecario in order for it to expand agricultural credit. Increased borrowing and increasing currency emission unleashed a ferocious and unforgiving inflation rate. From 1928 to 1938, the exchange rate increased from 5 sucres per U.S. dollar to 14.13 sucres per dollar, a 182.6% hike within a decade.

Financial tribulations were intrinsically connected to the cataclysmic conglomerate of ruin the country was in. The constant protests and public demands intensified in 1932 when an organized mob called the *Compactación Obrera* (workers' compaction) prepared daily incursions of street manifestations in the capital in support of Neptalí Bonifaz. As tensions increased, congress finally convened in August of 1932. However, congress did not validate the election from 1931 as had been expected. Rather it confirmed rumors that Bonifaz was to be disqualified as president-elect.

Born in Ecuador, Bonifaz was the son of a Peruvian diplomat, and although his mother was Ecuadorian, and even though he was an Ecuadorian for all practical purposes, he had held a Peruvian passport; as he put it, it was a "negligence of youth."[112] So, on the evening of August

---

[111] Rodriguez, *Government Finances and the Search for Public Policy*, 169.

[112] Dobronski, *El Ecuador: Los hechos más importantes de su historia*, 292.

20, 1932, after 10 days of futile negotiations between congress and Bonifaz, the legislature disqualified his candidacy and all hell broke loose. Seven days later, on August 27, 1932, the Compactación Obrera, otherwise known as the *Compactados*, with the support of several military battalions went up in arms against forces supporting congress. This resulted in *La Guerra de los Cuatro Días* (the Four Days' War), a bloody fratricidal conflict that took the lives of thousands of Ecuadorians. During this time of war, president Baquerizo Moreno, forced to resign by the nation's circumstances, did so on August 28th while naming Carlos Freile Larrea as Minister of State so that he could assume power after his resignation, as dictated by the constitution.

Three days later Ecuador was in a state of anarchy. There was no seated government as on September 1st, Freile Larrea resigned along with his war minister in order to follow a constitutional precept that stipulated that the new president was to take office that day, or new elections be convened (elections implied that responsibility lay with the head of congress). Nevertheless, an accord was finally reached around 7pm when Neptalí Bonifaz surrendered and retreated to his family hacienda. Alberto Guerrero Martinez, as the last president of the senate, assumed the office of president on September 2, the following day.

Three months later, Juan de Dios Martinez assumed the presidency. Only 10 months later he was deposed amidst worsening financial circumstances. Many politicians desired Ecuador go to war by entering the conflict of Leticia[113] between Colombia and Peru. When Martinez refused, congress issued a vote of distrust with the pretext that he was unable to adequately carry out the international businesses of the country. Two attempts to reconstitute the country, and ten other Ecuadorian heads of state (five acting presidents, two elected presidents, two supreme chiefs, and one interim president) would follow Juan de Dios Martinez during the difficult time of 1930s Ecuador. Then on September 1, 1940, Carlos Alberto Arroyo del Río would assume the presidency and serve the first complete term since José Luis Tamayo, who had served as president from 1920 through 1924.

---

[113] Armed conflict between Colombia and Peru that lasted from September 1, 1932, to May 24, 1933.

War

On July 17, 1936, the *pronunciamiento*[114] marked the start of the Spanish Civil War, marking the beginning of lasting conflict in Europe. Officially, the Second World War would come under way in 1939 after the Nazi invasion of Poland on September 1st. In Ecuador, armed conflict would begin almost two years later, on July 1941.

The economic and political context Ecuador had endured since the fall of the cacao trade, had assured the country be unable to effectively respond to foreign policy challenges and defend their national interests. This was painfully evidenced when Ecuador forfeited the legitimate and long-standing territorial claims of Amazonian territory to both Colombia and Peru as those nations battled for disputed ground, which included these Ecuadorian claims. Ecuador never entered into conflict, as it felt betrayed by Colombia when it had relinquished territories that had been Ecuadorian to Peru. Lacking the military might to square off against either Colombia or Peru, Ecuador remained neutral and acquiesced.

From September 1, 1932, to May 24, 1933, Colombia and Peru engaged in an armed conflict after Peru invaded the territory of Leticia. Peru was unsatisfied with the terms of the peace agreement, the Salomón-Lozano Treaty, reached 10 years prior and had thus decided to claim by force what they thought should be theirs. The incident was settled by the Rio de Janeiro Protocol of 1933, which ratified the Salomón-Lozano Treaty of 1922. Following the conflict with Colombia, in 1936, the Peruvian army, wanting to overturn their military discomfitures, advanced their military posts in the Amazon towards Ecuador. Pressured by this advance, and with a nonexistent military force, Ecuador signed the Ulloa-Viteri Accord, which set up a status quo line invented by Peru based on the effective possession of territory that each country had in the region at the time. In this accord, historical borders were virtually ignored and instead were the Peruvian military posts that determined country borders.

Meanwhile, Ecuador's financial troubles were aggravating all corners of the nation's problems. The incessant changes of heads of state resulted in a severely deficient diplomacy that, among other instances of negligence, had forgotten to join the League of Nations, and in September

---

114 Coup d'état proclaimed by a group of generals under the leadership of Spanish General José Sanjurjo against the elected government of the Second Spanish Republic.

1936 requested to directly negotiate with Peru the border disputes. This decision detached the mediation of the United States and left Ecuador alone to deal with its aggressive southern neighbor. By 1938, Ecuadorian president Manuel María Borrero requested the mediation of Argentina, Brazil, Chile, the United States, and Uruguay, to find a solution to the growing tensions of the border dispute. The request was rejected by Peru and any solution became moot.

What Ecuador desired most was access to the Marañón River. This wide and very navigable tributary of the Amazon meant Ecuador would assure access to both oceans. To this point, Ecuador was resolute. The country had already conceded too much of its territory throughout its 110-year history, principally to Brazil in 1904, Colombia in 1916; and to both Colombia and Peru in 1922 and again in 1933 when both countries negotiated the territories rightfully claimed by Ecuador. Peru, on the other hand, wanted vindication. Ecuador's southern neighbor had lost its territorial disputes to Chile in the War of the Pacific (1879-1883), and to Colombia in the conflict of Leticia. It wanted to redeem national pride through a profitable resolution with unstable Ecuador.

Peru's plan seems to have initiated at least since 1931, in preparation to fight with Colombia. From 1931 to 1941, Peru more than doubled its army, from 8,000 to 16,705 soldiers, and purchased fighters, bombers, and navy destroyers.[115] Further, it hosted a military mission from fascist Italy that lasted from 1937 to 1941, and continuous military cooperation with Japan during all the 1930s. Conversely, Ecuador did almost nothing to respond to Peru's army build-up and mobilizations (See supplement 1). The nation's severe financial and political problems during the 1930s meant that war with Peru was not at the forefront of the nation's to-do list. Ecuador held the belief that diplomacy would be the vehicle to solve the disputes with its southern neighbor and was thus unable to militarily respond to the Peruvian transgressions.

Ecuador was not prepared for war. During the hostilities between Colombia and Peru, the Ecuadorian budget was barely over 49 million sucres, and actual revenue under 42 million (See table 18). The cost to properly arm 20,000 men in 1933 was 25 million sucres, and the cost to finance them for six months exceeded 40 million. Towards the end of the decade, the situation had not changed much. Ecuador was still struggling

---

[115] Pineo, *Useful Strangers*, 1321.

financially as well as politically, and the nation's military was equally in distress. In 1940, the totality of Ecuador's reserves was 67,140,000 sucres, and even with two extraordinary budgets approved by congress that same year, the nation's budget never surpassed 122 million sucres ($7,261,904.76 with an exchange rate of 16.80 sucres per U.S. dollar). The military budgets were appalling, and in fact decreased from 1939 to 1941 (see table 23). The export-dependent economy suffered at the wake of the fighting in Europe and thus Ecuador was unable to effectively increase funds.

Table 23: Ecuador military budgets, 1939-1941[116]

Year	Amount in sucres
1939	29,414,044
1940	26,740,000
1941	24,676,930

By 1940, the war in Europe was the focus. As Winston Churchill replaced Neville Chamberlain as Prime Minister of the United Kingdom, Peruvian troops were advancing towards Ecuadorian territory. As Churchill delivered his famous "blood, toil, tears and sweat" speech, Peru was actively recruiting troops. Blood, toil, tears and sweat is what awaited Ecuador as they inexplicably diminished their military budget in November 1940 and 1941. On January 1941, Ecuador unsuccessfully requested that Peruvian troops withdraw. By February, the Peruvian invasion seemed imminent as they continued to advance with the pretext that Ecuador was mobilizing its own troops towards the Peruvian territory of Zarumilla. Three months later, Peru pressured the withdrawal of the mediation that had been offered by Argentina, Brazil, and the United States, as well as rejected the joint letter issued by the same countries urging an end to the dispute (Ecuador had immediately accepted both the mediation and the letter). Then, on July 5, 1941, with the pretext of protecting Peruvian farmers, hostilities broke out.

Peru, in fact, wanted war. Given the American continent's preoccupation with aggression from the Axis powers, Peruvian officials determined the time was right to invade. As Peruvian farmers crossed into Ecuadorian territory, border patrols began exchanging shots. The

[116]Academia Nacional De Historia Militar, comp., *Historia militar del Ecuador*, 444.

following day, Peru would launch an artillery attack and send over its bombers. The three-week war was a very uneven one. Peru's population was over twice as large as Ecuador's, Peru's national budget was over four times as large, and Peru's military budget was twelve times as large as Ecuador's. Peru invaded with over 13,000 troops while Ecuador defended with less than 2,000 ill-equipped soldiers.[117]

On July 22, Peru overturned Ecuadorian garrisons to advance into the province of El Oro. By July 26, Peruvian forces, aided by newly acquired Italian fighters and U.S. bombers, were reaching the Ecuadorian cities of Machala and Puerto Bolivar. In Guayaquil, Ecuadorian forces mutinied while in the occupied provinces the local population did nothing to resist the invaders. Ecuador's best fighting force, the *Cuerpo de Carabineros* (Rifle Corps) never made it to the border, as president Arroyo del Río kept them in Quito apparently in order to safeguard his unpopular regime. In point of fact, the Peruvian army did not really fight the Ecuadorian as such, but rather faint detachments of it since the bulk of the regular military remained in garrison throughout the country. Thus, by the end of July 1941, the Peruvian forces were decidedly imposing their strength on Ecuadorian soil while the Ecuadorian military cleared from the battlefield in defeat and openly disserting. Peru would suffer one hundred casualties from the war, but at least five hundred Ecuadorians died in battle.[118]

On July 26, 1941, Ecuador and Peru agreed to a cease-fire, although Peruvian forces continued their advance. In fact, Peruvian General and commander of the Peruvian armed forces, Eloy Ureta, pressured Lima for permission to advance all the way to Guayaquil. By August 2, the mediating nations advised a troop withdrawal, which Peru did not respond to. Ecuador accepted immediately. By September 15, Peru had occupied over 1000 square kilometers of Ecuadorian territory and demanded Ecuador immediately relinquish them control of it. Ecuador proposed an armistice, which Peru finally accepted on October 2, 1941. The following December, the mediating nations proposed a withdrawal of troops to the 1936 borderline, which again Ecuador agreed to immediately while Peru refused.

On January 1942, the Third Consultative Meeting of the Ministers of Foreign Affairs of the American Republics met in Rio de Janeiro. After the

---

[117] Pineo, *Useful Strangers*, 1339.

[118] Pineo, *Useful Strangers*, 1348.

Empire of Japan bombed Pearl Harbor on December 7, 1941, the United States had insistently called for the Rio de Janeiro conference in order to line up Latin American support for the allied war effort. In the meetings, Ecuador sought to have the Peruvian invasion treated as well, however, the U.S.-led conference considered the Ecuador-Peru war as a distraction given the much more pressing matters concerning the Axis powers. In fact, the Peruvians took this to their advantage, as they knew the United States would not come to the aid of Ecuador with fighting going on in Europe. In fact, Peru now demanded territories that had clearly been Ecuadorian, plus reparations.

Moreover, important financial interests within the disputed territory accompanied the snub to Ecuador's plight at the U.S.-led conference. In 1937, the Ecuadorian government had granted use of oil-rich lands to the Anglo Saxon Petroleum Company, a subsidiary of Royal Dutch Shell. Likewise, the Peruvian government had granted territories with presumed rich oil reserves to North American companies. This fact cannot be overlooked when analyzing the behavior of the United States in addressing the Ecuador-Peru conflict. With the Netherlands being occupied by Nazi Germany, Shell was now considered to be serving German interests and thus Allied efforts included diminishing the potential for oil exploitation in the "German" controlled Ecuadorian jungle. Likewise, the United States would have wanted to protect its own interests by having Peru gain more land because North American oil companies had agreements with the Peruvian government to make use of the perceived oil in those territories.[119] Further still, the United States was desperate to decrease Nazi presence in Latin America. From 1929 to 1936, German imports rose from 12% to 21% of Ecuador's total, with the U.S. falling from 40 to 27%.[120]

Meanwhile Peru, having ignored every petition to retreat, was still occupying Ecuadorian territory. Furthermore, it had given Ecuador a six-month deadline to surrender to their demands or face the consequences. Given the circumstances, the Ecuadorian government had no choice but to concede, if it did not, Peru would have probably pressed its military advantage to invade more territory. U.S. officials had no intent on

---

119 Jorge Villacres Moscoso, *Problemas económicos y políticos del Ecuador*, vol. 1 (Guayaquil: ESPOL, 1978), 113.

120 Pineo, *Useful Strangers*, 1405.

interfering and were focused on having this conflict end so that the continent could stand united against Axis aggression. Ecuador's efforts to get U.S. backing were futile. The nation's leading diplomatic representatives were sent to Washington and relations with the Axis powers broken, yet the United States would not entertain the Ecuadorian plight. In point of fact, the United States never tried to make a case against the Peruvian aggression even when Peru blatantly violated the cease-fire agreement, and damaged U.S. property through their aerial bombings. The official position of the United States to not endorse the seizing of territory by force of arms was forgotten, and Ecuador was left alone and defeated.

The shamelessly named *Protoclo de Paz, Amistad, y Límites* (Protocol of Peace, Friendship and Boundaries) was signed by Ecuadorian Foreign Minister Julio Tobar Donoso on January 29, 1942 in Rio de Janeiro with Argentina, Brazil, Chile, and the United States as guarantors. The treaty was a terrible deal for Ecuador; it forced the country to relinquish all territorial claims in the Amazon, claims that had been in existence since independence from Spain. Additionally, it relinquished over 200,000 square kilometers of territory to Peru, almost half the area of the entire country.[121] The treaty was ratified by Peru on February 26, 1942, fifteen days after it had started its retreat from occupied Ecuador. Ecuador followed; ratifying the protocol on February 27, 1942, after the senate had approved it four days earlier with 26 votes in favor, 3 against and 5 abstentions.

Nine months later, on November 1942, Franklin Delano Roosevelt tried to make amends by inviting Arroyo del Río to Washington (he had done the same with the Peruvian president in May). When he arrived, both Roosevelt and vice-president Henry Wallace greeted him at the airport and honored him with a banquet at the White House. He was then granted the opportunity to address Congress, and later received honorary degrees from Columbia and George Washington University. Nevertheless, the damage was done and most Ecuadorians felt betrayed even when a generous local press celebrated the president's trip, which had been a first of its kind for a sitting Ecuadorian head of state. Trips to Colombia, Cuba, Mexico, Panama and Venezuela were also carried out that year.

---

[121] Total area of Ecuador as of 1998 is 275,830 square kilometers.

For two years following his visit to the United States, Arroyo del Río held a grip on power using force on all political opponents, real or imagined as these may have been. His trustworthy battalion of Carabineros managed to suppress several uprisings during this time, including an armed assault on the presidential palace on May 1943. However, by 1944, growing discontent was further fueled when, as election time approached, Arroyo del Río faithful Miguel Angel Albornoz was handpicked to be the president's successor. This resulted in a massive opposition movement called the *Alianza Democrática Ecuatoriana* with former president Velasco Ibarra (1934-1935, 1944-1947, 1952-1956, 1960-1961, 1968-1972), who was exiled in Chile, as the sole opposing candidate. When Arroyo del Río tried to forbid Velasco's return to Ecuador, and bizarrely cede more territory (the island of Matapalo) to Peru, public clamor for action continued to increase. Then on May 28, 1944, factions of the military in Guayaquil staged a successful uprising that quickly spread throughout the country with the support of thousands of people. After lamentable fighting, which resulted in the death of many Ecuadorians, Arroyo del Río resigned and fled to the United States in disgrace. The uprising was enthusiastically named *La Gloriosa*, which can in fact be viewed as a glorious effort that restored national pride after the dreadful blow of the Rio de Janeiro Protocol.

As it happened, Ecuador's financial fallout started a series of events that ended with the greatest tragedy in the nation's history. The country could never recover from the demise of the cacao trade, and the turbulent decade of the world financial crisis could not be controlled. From 1931 to 1940, no less than fifteen heads of state and twenty ministers of finance tried to lead Ecuador. The financial ruin assured Ecuador was unable to maintain political stability, which in turn severely affected all diplomatic efforts. Further, it became impossible to fund a proper military that could have been prepared for war.

As the United States war effort pulled that economy out of the Great Depression, the strategic decisions to consolidate U.S. presence in Latin America bonded the economies of Ecuador and the United States. As in World War I, the United States took over the decreasing exports to Europe. Further fueled by escalating wartime spending, the United States acquired a virtual monopsony of Ecuadorian goods. Panama hats, balsa wood, and rubber exports significantly increased. Further, as the U.S. diminished trade with Japan in protest of Japan's expansionist actions, culminating with a complete embargo on July 1941, Ecuador took over and became a leading supplier of rice to the United States (see table 24). By 1944, rice was Ecuador's leading export, representing 27.5% of all exportations. In all, Ecuador's exports to the United States increased from $7.5 million in 1939 to $28.6 million in 1944; Ecuador's imports increased from $11.2 million in 1939 to $24 million in 1945.[122]

Table 24: Selected Ecuadorian exports as a percent of total value, 1939-1945[123]

Year	Cacao	Coffee	Rice	P. Hats	Crude Oil	Balsa	Rubber
1939	22.1	9.1	4.0	3.0	14.4	1.7	2.6
1940	17.5	9.8	8.7	3.9	14.8	1.9	2.3
1941	17.2	11.9	11.6	8.1	6.7	4.2	3.5
1942	13.5	5.8	17.2	7.4	8.3	8.6	11.9
1943	13.2	11.0	24.1	6.4	6.1	11.0	5.9
1944	9.0	9.3	27.5	14.8	6.2	6.8	8.2
1945	14.2	11.3	16.0	18.4	7.4	4.9	6.2

Ironically, Ecuador's financial situation improved in the immediate aftermath of the war with Peru. The U.S. economic machine that originated with the war effort tagged Ecuador along with increased trade between both nations. Long sought-after foreign capital came in the 1940s when an Export-Import Bank loan to Ecuador was granted for the building of the Pan-American Highway. The North Americans also constructed military bases in Salinas and Galapagos. Customs revenue as a percentage of national income steadily increased throughout World War II with the exception of 1941 where decreased oil exports signified a decrease in customs revenue, perhaps due to the issues regarding Royal Dutch Shell in the oil-rich regions of the Ecuadorian Amazon during the conflict with Peru (see table 25). With customs revenue, government income also increased during the war years (see table 26).

[122] Pineo, *Useful Strangers*, 1439.

[123] Rodriguez, *Government Finances and the Search for Public Policy*, 180-181.

Table 25: Customs revenue as a percentage of national government income, 1939-1945[124]

Year	Absolute Amount in sucres	% of national income
1939	35,571,000	30
1940	43,518,000	40
1941	38,709,000	36
1942	53,398,000	41
1943	67,501,000	40
1944	95,237,000	45
1945	90,203,000	36

Table 26: National government income, 1939-1946[125]

Year	Absolute Amount in sucres	Year	Absolute Amount in sucres
1939	117,187,000	1943	168,284,000
1940	108,533,000	1944	211,958,000
1941	109,001,000	1945	252,717,000
1942	128,985,000	1946	298,813,000

However, as World War II came to an end in 1945, so did the benefits of commerce with the United States. Moreover, the Velasco government's complete disregard for fiscal discipline and even a blatant case of misappropriation of funds, in which Velasco himself, with no proper authorization, made use of $6.5 million from the Central Bank with the pretext of directing them to pressing public works projects, resulted in a bloated and corrupt bureaucracy.[126] The misallocation of funds that was well underway, usually with the ploy of funding public works projects, was reminiscent of the pre-Kemmerer liberal era. The irresponsible patterns of Ecuadorian politics returned with force as the economy started to recover during World War II.

And so, as Japan surrendered after receiving the wrath of two atomic bombs, Ecuador once again suffered the effects of a weak economy. To keep up with fiscal indiscipline the Velasco government simply printed more bills, causing devastating inflation yet again for Ecuador. After a quarrel between the president and his minister of Defense, Colonel Carlos

---

[124] Rodriguez, *Government Finances and the Search for Public Policy*, 189.

[125] Rodriguez, *Government Finances and the Search for Public Policy*, 220.

[126] Academia Nacional De Historia Militar, comp., *Historia militar del Ecuador*, 489.

Mancheno Cajas, rumors began circulating that the minister would be deposed. The colonel, beating the president to the punch, took up arms against Velasco and forced him to resign on August 24, 1947, a day properly known in Ecuadorian history as *El Manchenazo.*

With efforts aimed at keeping constitutional rule, colonel Mancheno supported the succession of Vice-president Mariano Suarez Veintimilla after himself acting as supreme chief for ten days. On September 2, 1947, Suarez Veintimilla would assume the role of acting president of Ecuador and immediately organized elections in parliament for a new head of state. On September 17, with the principal objective of organizing general elections, Carlos Julio Arosemena Tola assumed the presidency until August 31, 1948. The end of Velasco Ibarra's second presidency and subsequent re-organization of politics in Ecuador marked the end of the Age of Crises in the country.

Picture 11: Liga Militar poster

Picture 12: Heads of First Provisional Government, 1925.

Picture 13: Luis Napoleon Dillon.

Picture 14: Ecuadorian soldiers marching to the front in 1941.

Chapter 3
The Banana Republic (1948-1972)

On June 6, 1948, the Republic of Ecuador observed general presidential elections. With a tight margin, Galo Plaza Lasso defeated Manuel Elicio Flor to become president of Ecuador. With the country on stable constitutional rule, Ecuador also began to benefit from an improving economy, although admittedly with intermittent reverses along the way. In the decades following the Second World War, Ecuador enjoyed economic growth, with its average annual GDP growth being 5.03% from 1948 to 1972, a growth rate faster than that of most Latin American nations, and even better than that of the world's economic superpower, the United States of America (3.83% from 1948 to 1972).[127] From 1948 to 1970, government income continually increased at an average rate of 10.44% per year, as did customs revenue with an average yearly growth rate of 12.32% from 1948 to 1972.

Chiefly during this time, however, was the ever-increasing production of the fruits from the herbaceous plants of the genus *Musa*, otherwise known as bananas. Measured by amount in metric tons, banana exports grew an astounding 1240% from 1948 to 1970 (see table 27), making Ecuador the world's foremost producer of the fruit. Once again, Ecuador would become a world superpower of an agricultural commodity. This time however, it was bananas, not cacao, that would earn the country the distinction. With another commodity boom, Ecuador would start the second half of the 20th century with a similar optimism as the one it had started the first half of the century with. Like the cacao age, the banana bonanza would come and go, yet unlike the demise of the Ecuadorian cacao export economy that obliterated the nation's finances, Ecuador would continue on being a world banana superpower into the 21st century.

---

[127] Calculated from figures published by *The Groningen Growth and Development Centre.*

Table 27: Banana exports 1948-1972[128]

Year	Metric Tons	U.S. Dollars x 1000[129]	% of total exports
1948	99,634	2,761	6.9
1949	137,988	4,944	16.7
1950	169,625	7,854	12.8
1951	246,454	11,252	20.0
1952	429,820	21,380	26.7
1953	406,363	23,674	31.3
1954	492,151	27,671	27.4
1955	612,615	36,761	41.1
1956	578,915	36,505	39.3
1957	669,063	34,520	35.0
1958	742,743	33,848	50.9
1959	885,571	44,261	63.0
1960	895,053	45,267	60.8
1961	842,342	48,005	63.4
1962	897,832	62,306	58.0
1963	1,014,340	67,833	53.0
1964	1,172,474	68,951	52.8
1965	874,580	49,997	38.5
1966	1,070,665	59,393	46.6
1967	1,145,699	67,158	44.0
1968	1,259,151	92,219	41.7
1969	1,173,884	68,175	43.8
1970	1,335,055	83,229	46.8
1971		88,157	
1972		130,991	

During the onset of the banana-fueled economy, Ecuador experienced stability and progress. Ecuador, in effect, went bananas. Infrastructure was built, and the country attempted to industrialize the economy. Before this product, the country had a virtually nonexistent highway system. But from 1944 to 1967, the Ecuadorian government built over 3,500 kilometers of highway, almost doubling the amount of roads throughout the country.[130] Likewise, port infrastructure was built in order to accommodate the increasing banana trade, which by 1951 had become

[128] Rodriguez, *Government Finances and the Search for Public Policy*, 200.

[129] *Indices económicos del Ecuador. Country Statistics*. Accessed February 1, 2012. https://www.bce.fin.ec/documentos/PublicacionesNotas/Catalogo/Anuario/80anios/indice.htm.

[130] Pineo, *Useful Strangers*, 1631.

Ecuador's most important export, and which by 1959 represented 63% of total exportations. Government was able to acquire stability, and just as it had happened with cacao, society became organized around the nation's chief export. Essentially, the evolution of the Ecuadorian banana industry shaped all aspects of the country's life: political, social, and naturally, financial. Ultimately, Ecuador would become a banana monoculture, a banana republic.

The United Fruit Company

The United Fruit Company was a multinational corporation that formed in 1899 as a result of the merger engagements between Minor C. Keith and Andrew W. Preston. Together with the Standard Fruit Company, the company would come to control the international banana industry with a remarkable network of plantations in Latin America and distribution channels throughout the world. It could be said that Ecuador owes its second commodity explosion of the 20th century to the United Fruit Company. At the very least, it can be stated that United Fruit's period in Ecuador corresponded with the banana boom in the country. As former Ecuadorian president Galo Plaza Lasso asserted in 1958,

> The United Fruit Company, since its incorporation in 1899, has played the leading role of pioneer in almost every stage of development that has made this trade feasible—from large-scale plantation production, through disease control techniques, land and ocean transport, and sales promotion. Without the United Fruit Company's initiative, it is highly unlikely that the world trade in bananas would have developed to anything approaching its present dimension.[131]

In point of fact, from 1900 through to the 1960s, every phase of the global banana industry was operated with the direct involvement of multinational corporations. Companies like the United Fruit Company and Standard Fruit carried out all aspects of banana production, transportation, and distribution. Their operation consisted in acquiring

---

[131] Stacy May and Galo Plaza Lasso, *The United Fruit Company in Latin America* (New York: Arno Press, 1976), 220.

immense tracts of land and creating a human settlement around a banana plantation. In these vast estates, often referred to as enclaves, they would make huge investments in machinery, infrastructure, and other resources, in order to produce the fruit that would subsequently be sold in the prime markets of the United States and Europe.

During the beginning of the banana industry, which more or less took place during the first three decades of the 20th century, there were a number of circumstances that made it possible for the entire industry to spawn out of the direct involvement of powerful multinational corporations. The purchasing of large quantities of land that were subsequently cleared for planting, the development of extensive canals, construction of railroads, purchasing of machinery, scientific research, and overall the global transportation and distribution procedures of a perishable commodity, required investments that surpassed the capacity of most capitalists. Henceforth, by 1930, the United Fruit Company became the undisputed ruler of the global banana industry with assets close to $250 million (equal to $3.4 billion in 2012).[132]

Furthermore, this process had to be repeated on a regular basis. The ease with which banana plantations depleted the soil, and their vulnerability to disease, meant that corporations operated in a semi-migratory mode. Companies like United Fruit repeatedly moved from one site to the next. From 1900 to 1910 the company's most extensive plantations were located in Costa Rica and Panama. When the Panama Disease[133] destroyed production in both these countries, United Fruit packed up and went searching for other locations in other countries where disease was absent. The company set up enclaves in several nations, such as Colombia, Guatemala, Honduras, and Mexico.

The various enclaves of production that United Fruit operated helped the company diminish the risk not only of plant disease, but also of an unruly workforce. If at any point a certain country operation experienced a strike, United Fruit, confident that production would continue from its various plantations, simply waited until the protests ended.[134] However, even with the mitigation of risk, United Fruit began to experience pressure

---

[132] Striffler, *In the Shadows of State and Capital*, 31.

[133] Plant disease that affects the roots of banana plants.

[134] These strikes included infamous episodes like the Banana Massacre on November 12, 1928 on the Caribbean coast of Colombia.

from governments and workers during the 1930s. No longer was the company able to acquire generous land concessions or tax breaks, as labor laws strengthened in practically all banana-producing nations of the time. Thus, out of the need to find disease-free land and a passive workforce, the United Fruit Company entered Ecuador in 1934 when the company decided to purchase the famous Hacienda Tenguel.

At first glance, Ecuador seemed like the ideal place for United Fruit to expand its operations. Labor organizations were relatively underdeveloped and the country's agricultural land was largely desolate as a result of the demise of cacao. Consequently, when United Fruit began exploring the Ecuadorian coast for suitable land they found vast terrains, of what had been cacao plantations, available and disease-free. Furthermore, the existence of extensive tracts of tropical lowlands with first-rate forest soils and terrific precipitation levels attracted plantation experts.[135] Even more, the country's equatorial location assured that destructive hurricanes, that had decimated plantations in Central America, would not be an issue. Chiefly among all lands explored was Tenguel. The 100,000 hectare hacienda, which had spearheaded the cacao bonanza, would now become United Fruit's Ecuadorian headquarters.

When United Fruit arrived at Tenguel in 1934, the country was exporting 35,987 metric tons of bananas, which represented 2% of the nation's total exports.[136] The once fertile cacao zone lay abandoned with neglected cacao trees and a growing jungle terrain. Further, the troubled governments of the post-cacao age had done next to nothing to connect the country with roads. Guayaquil, which in the 1930s had grown to become a dynamic city of 100,000 people, was still more than a day's journey from hacienda Tenguel (currently about a two-hour drive), and other important would-be centers of production were not even on maps. Machala, the future banana capital of the world, was accessible only by small boats during the 1930s (currently, it is a less than 3-hour drive from Guayaquil, and less than a one-hour drive from Tenguel).[137]

Consequently, United Fruit transformed everything. It cleared up the jungle and made it suitable for banana production. It built a railroad

---

[135] With exceptions, annual precipitation exceeds 100 inches in most of the Ecuadorian rainforest that lies between the Andes and the Pacific Ocean.

[136] Rodriguez, *Government Finances and the Search for Public Policy*, 200.

[137] Striffler, *In the Shadows of State and Capital*, 41.

system that covered the cultivated portions of the hacienda, rebuilt the entire town of Tenguel, and even expanded the populated areas to other corners of the immense property. Everything was brought in, from the wood used in construction to all the employees and workers, who were procured from United Fruit's Central American operations and from other parts of Ecuador. The town of Tenguel, where the hacienda workers resided, included a church, a first-rate hospital, a movie theater, clubhouses for both workers and administrative employees, and the Tenguel port that served to transport fruit out of the hacienda, and the ever-growing number of construction materials in.

After World War II, Hacienda Tenguel had its infrastructure ready and its banana plantations rising. Thousands of hectares of fruit were rooted, so when the worldwide demand for bananas exploded, Tenguel was ready to meet the requirement and quickly became the largest producer of the fruit in the country. Thousands of workers were hired to meet the demands of the hacienda's infrastructure and increasing plantations. By the late 1940s, Tenguel employed over 2000 workers that handled over 80,000 stems of bananas every week. Eventually, Tenguel under United Fruit would employ 3500 workers out of which 1500 had families living with them at the central town and at the surrounding settlements in San Rafael, La Esperanza, Pagua, Chimborazo, and Cotopaxi.[138]

Needless to say, even with the hacienda existing in relative isolation from the rest of the country, Tenguel's massive investments and substantial workforce propelled the Ecuadorian southern coast into rapid development. The company's presence demanded regional markets and infrastructure to function, and it was not long before entrepreneurs and workers from all over the country noticed and took advantage of the opportunities the vast influx of capital was generating. Eventually, this sphere of influence would spread throughout Ecuador as the banana industry swiftly developed during the presidency of Galo Plaza Lasso.

Reform and Infrastructure

The son of former Ecuadorian president Leonidas Plaza, Galo Plaza was born during his father's exile in 1906 in New York City, at the famous

---

[138] Striffler, *In the Shadows of State and Capital*, 42.

Marlton House.[139] Educated in the United States, he studied agriculture at the University of Maryland, economics at the University of California, Berkeley, and diplomacy at Georgetown University. His political career began when he was elected as alderman of Quito in 1936, and mayor two years later. After exercising other posts like that of Minister of War, he successfully assumed the office of president of Ecuador on September 1, 1948.

From the start, Galo Plaza approached government with a progressive and technocratic emphasis. His interaction with international advisors was evident from the start. Just as the Ecuadorian government had relied on Edwin Kemmerer during the 1920s, Galo Plaza sent for experts from various organizations and nationalities. Specialists from the International Monetary Fund, the Export-Import Bank, UNICEF, UNESCO, the Organization of American States, ECLAC, among others, arrived in Ecuador to help Plaza organize his government. His favorability to capitalist endeavors propelled the Ecuadorian economy to buoyant levels, his staunch support of the rule of law and liberty transformed Ecuadorian society to the degree that his actions still resonate today. As the Organization of American States' 2006 commemoration of Galo Plaza's 100th birthday highlights:

> Mr. Galo Plaza Lasso during his four years of government, demonstrated profound democratic convictions and exemplified a paragon of tolerance, full respect for human rights and freedom of expression, and also in this same period he made extensive public works and promoted a visionary economic policy that made Ecuador the leading Banana exporter in the world.

Accordingly, his support towards the United Fruit Company could not have been any better.

Previously, during the troubled 1930s, the United Fruit Company experienced difficulties with government relations. Even though it played decisive roles in United Fruit's ability to purchase land, export production, and control peasant workers, the government's actions were "ambiguous, contradictory, and divided because the state itself was so fragmented."[140]

---

[139] Located on 5 West 8th Street in Greenwich Village, the Marlton House (also known as the Hotel Marlton) in Manhattan is notable for having been the residence of several famous personalities, principally writers and poets.

[140] Striffler, *In the Shadows of State and Capital*, 30.

Conflicts and legislation were rarely carried out in an organized and coherent manner, fact that severely hindered United Fruit's ability to function properly. Even with the resources United Fruit had at its disposal, the situation of the Ecuadorian government was in such disarray that the company could not predict or control the actions that would be taken. In other words, the Ecuadorian government's weakness and instability made it impossible for capitalists to function outside the realm of the nationwide chaos.

So when President Plaza took office, the stabilization of the economy, which had begun improving since the latter years of the Second World War, allowed this president to enact reforms that would catapult Ecuador into its second commodity-fueled bonanza of the 20th century. In 1947, bananas was a minor factor in the Ecuadorian economy with only 2.7 million stems of fruit being exported. By 1955, however, Ecuador exported 23.9 million stems cultivated from the more than 114,000 hectares of planted farmland.[141] In less than a decade, Ecuador increased the number of stems exported by a factor of over 785%. This development owes much of its success to the reforms enacted and public works projects constructed by the government presided by Plaza.

One of the first laws passed during this administration was the *Ley de Fomento de la Producción* (Law on the Promotion of Production). This law promoted agriculture, and local industry, which resulted in the importation of several goods to become unnecessary due to the development of local productiveness. It also promoted the colonization of undeveloped lands (*baldíos*), as well as the purchase and division of large estates among willing private entities. Further, through the direction of finance minister Clemente Yerovi Indaburo, the state reorganized and transferred important enterprises to private companies, such as with the *Fábrica de Cemento de Chimborazo*, the *Repobladora de Banano y Cacao*, among others. The message sent was clear, government support to businesses was a priority.

Specifically with the banana trade, the Plaza government eliminated export taxes on the fruit, and installed a favorable government policy towards the industry. Export duties on bananas had crushed earlier ventures, and these had to be eliminated to take advantage of the growing

[141] May and Lasso, *The United Fruit Company in Latin America*, 169.

market for the fruit.[142] With regards to production, a significant impetus to banana planting was the government's liberal credit policy. From 1948 to 1951, loans where granted to nearly 1000 settlers through the *Banco Nacional de Fomento,*[143] which financed the planting of over 10,000 hectares of new banana plants.[144]

Galo Plaza was a great admirer of the United States, and he made no effort to hide his inclinations. In point of fact, as an admirer of president Franklin Roosevelt, the Plaza administration grounded economic policy on aspects of the New Deal. Perhaps the greatest example of this is President Plaza's focus on government action in public works projects. In fact, the most ambitious road-building program since Alfaro's railroad began in the late 1940s with the Daule-Quevedo, and Durán-Tambo highways. These projects, largely financed by the United States government, initiated a period in which the country would become connected through increasing roads and services. The Quito-Santo Domingo highway was also started, and its extensions to the navigable Esmeraldas River at Quinindé eventually opened up fertile lands for homesteaders. New roads in the provinces of El Oro and Manabí also succeeded in supplanting outdated pathways in order to achieve the task of moving bananas to tidewater.

Bonanza

With the foundations in place, Ecuador was positioned to become the worldwide banana superpower. As demand for bananas increased, Panama disease forced the change of the most commonly grown cultivar of banana from the Gros Michel (Big Mike) to the now well-known Cavendish. In Ecuador, United Fruit and its production of Cavendish bananas in Hacienda Tenguel were headlining the banana boom. Beginning in the late 1940s, and until the late 1950s, Tenguel became the largest single producer of bananas in Ecuador. At its peak, Tenguel

---

142 James J. Parsons, "Bananas in Ecuador: A New Chapter in the History of Tropical Agriculture," *Economic Geography* 33, no. 3 (July 1957): 201-216. Accessed June 17, 2012. http://www.jstor.org/stable/142308, 203.

143 The *Banco de Fomento* was formed in 1943 after the renaming and restructuring of the *Banco Hipotecario*

144 Parsons, "Bananas in Ecuador," 206.

employed thousands of workers and exported over 80,000 stems of bananas a week.[145]

Yet, the majority of United Fruit's business would come from the marketing and distribution of the fruit. In contrast to what had happened in Central America, where large multinationals grew most of the banana plants, in Ecuador, the fruit was mostly grown on small and medium-sized farms. In point of fact, by 1955 there were an estimated 40,000 farms.[146] By 1964, Ecuador would have about 3,000 banana farms averaging at about 64 hectares in size. Actually, United Fruit never surpassed five percent of the nation's total banana production,[147] but by 1954, 50% of Ecuador's banana exports were handled by only three companies, Standard Fruit, United Fruit, and the Ecuadorian Bananera Noboa.[148] During 1955, United Fruit purchased 3.8 million stems in the Ecuadorian market (the only exporting area where such substantial amounts of bananas could be purchased on an open market), which together with the company's own 1.3 million stems, represented just over 20% of the nation's total banana exports.[146] These three corporations thus laid claim to the greater part of the banana industry's profits by handling marketing and distribution and leaving all the risks of production to the actual banana farmers.

In 1955, the estimated 40,000 farms were assessed to be producing out of 115,000 hectares of planted bananas. This was more than twice the entire planted area United Fruit boasted in all of its Central and South American plantations combined. This signified that Ecuador was exporting 23.9 million stems, almost nine times more than what the country had exported in 1947. This represented almost three-fifths of the nation's exports that year, surpassing three times the amount of the nation's second leading export, coffee[146]. The 612,615 metric tons of fruit

---

[145] Striffler, *In the Shadows of State and Capital*, 83.

[146] May and Lasso, *The United Fruit Company in Latin America*, 169-170.

[147] Pineo, *Useful Strangers*, 1639.

[148] Exporters usually bought bananas from independent producers in three ways: 1. The Exporters agent bought bananas ready for shipment on the farm; 2. an independent buyer bought small quantities of bananas from a large number of small farms and usually arranged for shipment to the port where they were sold shipside; and 3. the exporter bought bananas at shipside, which farmers had transported to that point.

that left Ecuador's pacific shores in 1955 also increased customs revenue to represent 56% of ordinary government income (see table 28), consequently also increasing actual national government income to 739,202,000 sucres (see table 29), an increase of 64.7% and 98% respectively with relation to 1948. It also did not hurt that the price of bananas continually increased from 1948 to 1955 (see table 30), during this time the price per metric ton of bananas increased at a rate of almost one percent per year adjusted for inflation (a rate of 7% from 1948 with respect to 1955).

Table 28: Customs revenue as a percentage of national government income, 1948-1972[149]

Year	Absolute Amount x 1000	% of Government Income
1948	125,539	34
1949	130,121	33
1950	171,882	44
1951	204,570	47
1952	228,881	50
1953	308,000	55
1954	536,029	50
1955	567,697	56
1956	491,721	43
1957	575,937	43
1958	578,603	42
1959	587,692	44
1960	651,347	46
1961	750,996	48
1962	772,557	48
1963	938,397	51
1964	1,048,000	50
1965	958,000	48
1966	1,092,000	50
1967	1,442,832	55
1968	1,513,479	59
1969	1,545,000	52
1970	2,034,000	55
1971	2,225,000	50
1972	2,417,000	44

[149] Rodriguez, *Government Finances and the Search for Public Policy*, 189-190.

Table 29: National government income, 1948-1970[150]

Year	Absolute Amount in sucres x 1000	Year	Absolute Amount in sucres x 1000
1948	373,403	1960	916,678
1949	390,648	1961	1,564,505
1950	388,685	1962	1,622,727
1951	438,207	1963	1,843,786
1952	454,639	1964	2,460,628
1953	561,176	1965	2,535,712
1954	616,844	1966	2,146,946
1955	739,202	1967	2,632,223
1956	768,793	1968	2,922,649
1957	802,454	1969	3,356,000
1958	851,215	1970	3,716,000
1959	858,975		

150 Rodriguez, *Government Finances and the Search for Public Policy*, 220-221.

Table 30: Banana prices at U.S.A. ports per metric ton[151]

Year	Price in USD (Nominal)	% Period Change	Price in USD (Real)
1948	138.56	2.89	574.94
1949	153.51	14.95	650.47
1950	160.39	6.88	641.56
1951	160.39	0	605.25
1952	162.59	2.2	608.95
1953	162.59	0	604.42
1954	167.08	4.49	625.77
1955	164.87	-2.21	615.19
1956	167.08	2.21	605.36
1957	175.83	8.75	619.12
1958	162.59	-13.24	562.60
1959	145.05	-17.54	493.37
1960	142.84	-2.21	479.33
1961	138.47	-4.37	461.57
1962	131.9	-6.57	433.88
1963	167.08	35.18	540.71
1964	169.27	2.19	542.53
1965	158.21	-11.06	497.52
1966	153.81	-4.4	467.51
1967	158.21	4.4	466.70
1968	151.63	-6.58	427.13
1969	158.21	6.58	419.66
1970	164.87	6.66	414.25
1971	140.65	-24.22	342.21
1972	160.39	19.74	377.39

With these circumstances, Ecuador was once again in the midst of a huge commodity boom. As money came rolling in, Ecuador was able to achieve financial and political stability. President Galo Plaza was the first head of state in nearly 30 years to finish a complete term, something that had not occurred since José Luis Tamayo's 1920-1924 presidential period. The Ecuadorian people were happy. Not even after the shattering series of natural disasters in 1949 and 1950 was the rule of law interrupted. Finances permitted the Plaza government to rebuild Ambato and Latacunga after the devastating 1949 earthquake, and even organize a national census in 1950 after recovering.

---

[151] "Bananas US Ports." Global Financial Database. Accessed June 27, 2012. https://www.globalfinancialdata.com/.

Further, the buoyant economy allowed for foreign loans to be granted. These were obtained principally from the Export-Import Bank. During the banana bonanza several public works projects like new port facilities for Guayaquil, airports for Quito and Guayaquil, power plants, road construction, farming development, sheep raising initiatives, African Palm production, fishing industry development, cattle raising development, a program for the colonization of the Amazon provinces, and even a new hotel in Quito so that the country be able to host a meeting of the Organization of American States were built with the aid of these loans. After Plaza, Velasco Ibarra would become president for a third time (1952-1956) and stably serve a complete term as well. With the nation's financials improving, Velasco Ibarra continued building roads and schools across the country, as well as investing in irrigation systems in arid farmlands.

Financial stability also coincided with an era of improved Ecuadorian diplomacy. The financially wrenched period, in which the Ecuadorian military and diplomacy were in shambles, had resulted in the 1942 Rio Protocol, which inflicted a deep wound into Ecuadorians as they saw over 200,000 km of national territory being surrendered to Peru. By the mid 1940s the *Neutral Multistate Boundary Commission* had marked about 95% of the new border, and the United States offered to carry out the necessary aerial photographic survey of the remaining seventy-six kilometers of rough jungle territory left to demarcate. This dangerous and difficult task cost the lives of fourteen Americans, but the mapping was completed and the final report was submitted in February 1947.[152]

The report brought the Rio Protocol back into the headlines. The U.S. aerial survey had revealed a different course of the Cenepa River than what had up until then been thought. It also revealed a mountain spur, the *Cordillera del Cóndor.* This produced important geographic inconsistencies, which meant that the 1942 treaty was flawed. As a result, Ecuador would declare the unenforceability of the Rio Protocol, a position that would stand until financial necessity would once again force the

---

[152] Pineo, *Useful Strangers*, 1735.

nation to concede.[153] Furthermore, improved relations between Ecuador and the United States resulted in President Plaza visiting the United States in June of 1951 at the invitation of President Harry Truman.

Although bananas would continue to be an integral export product for Ecuador into the 21st century, the seven years from 1948 to 1955 can be considered the years in which the banana export economy exploded. The boom had brought extreme commercial success to United Fruit, Standard Fruit, and Bananera Noboa, out of which the wealthiest man in Ecuadorian history, Luis Noboa Naranjo, amassed his fortune. Other businesses involved with the banana industry also benefitted from the windfall the fruit produced, as did the economy in general. GDP and GDP per capita increased at an annual rate of 5.04% and 1.59% respectively during these years (see table 31).

[153] Ecuador had refused to sign the 1947 Rio Pact because it contained a clause in which it was stated that treaties between nations could be modified only with the consent of the parties involved, and Ecuador wanted out of the "unfair" Rio Protocol of 1942. However, Ecuador eventually signed the accord in 1950 when the United States informed the country that it would not receive any funds of the $1.5 billion foreign aid bill unless Ecuador joined the Rio Pact.

Table 31: GDP levels 1948-1972[154]

Year	GDP	Per Capita GDP
1948	5,673	1,880
1949	5,776	1,861
1950	6,278	1,863
1951	6,346	1,835
1952	7,129	2,009
1953	7,279	1,998
1954	7,867	2,103
1955	8,074	2,101
1956	8,373	2,121
1957	8,751	2,156
1958	9,007	2,159
1959	9,490	2,211
1960	10,106	2,289
1961	10,360	2,279
1962	10,911	2,331
1963	11,189	2,320
1964	11,977	2,411
1965	13,131	2,566
1966	13,475	2,556
1967	14,188	2,612
1968	14,973	2,675
1969	15,792	2,739
1970	16,899	2,845
1971	17,872	2,922
1972	18,972	3,012

[154] Angus Maddison, *Historical Statistics of the World Economy: 1-2008 AD.* Historical Statistics Report. Accessed June 17, 2012.

Reverses Within Prosperity and Stability

José María Velasco Ibarra was triumphant in a free general election organized in 1952. He was elected to succeed Galo Plaza with 153,934 votes, the highest ever count for a candidate. He had famously proclaimed, "Dadme un balcón en cada pueblo y triunfaré" (Give me a balcony in every town and I will win), and that is exactly what he did in order to assume his third presidency. The salubrious state of the Ecuadorian economy assured healthy government coffers and a stable presidency at the start of his third presidential term. Velasco was able to continue with the public works projects, which had been made possible due to the increase in government revenue of 11.3% a year from 1945 to 1955.[155]

However, his populist campaigns aimed at punishing the oligarchy and fighting for the disadvantaged resonated little once he assumed office. In fact, his government became notorious for repressing demonstrations with often-brutal force. During his mandate, as had been customary during his previous administrations, Velasco started many public works projects and increased bureaucracy. Most of these projects, however, never prospered and were left abandoned shortly after their first-stone ceremonies. Many funds were also spent on military buildup, such as with the purchases of several Douglas C-47 Skytrains and two modern destroyers, the *Presidente Alfaro,* and the *Presidente Velasco Ibarra.* The banana economy was healthy, but Velasco's spending habits were dwindling the hopes for economic consolidation. During Velasco's presidency, government expenditure increased at an average annual rate of 14.7%, conflicting with the 11.3% annual increase of government income. In contrast, the increase in government expenditure during the final year of the Plaza administration, from 1951 to 1952, was 6.7% (see table 32). Even though GDP continued to increase during Velasco's administration, the rapid escalation in expenditure seems to not have been necessary, and rather should have been avoided.

---

[155] Pineo, *Useful Strangers,* 1715.

Table 32: Government expenditure, 1950-1970[156]

Year	Expenditure (millions of sucres)	Year	Expenditure (millions of sucres)
1950	427.1	1961	1,687.0
1951	548.3	1962	1,581.0
1952	586.5	1963	1,647.0
1953	708.8	1964	2,110.0
1954	920.4	1965	2,405.0
1955	1,162.5	1966	2,725.0
1956	1,057.5	1967	3,230.0
1957	1,060.6	1968	3,418.0
1958	1,094.2	1969	3,931.0
1959	1,197.6	1970	4,662.0
1960	1,466.0		

In 1955, expenditure had squeezed the nation's treasury and the government was keen on continuing to build public works projects. As a Memorandum of an August 1955 conversation between Ecuadorian ambassador to the United States, Jose Chiriboga, and the United States Department of State describes, the Ecuadorian government was "anxious to obtain an Eximbank loan of $900,000 for terminal buildings at Guayaquil and Quito, stressing the fact that the present Government has only one year to go and wished to start this project before its term expires."[157] By 1956, the final year of Velasco Ibarra's third term, the banana boom was slowing down and the government was heading towards bankruptcy. Though the nation's internal public debt was reduced during the Plaza administration, from 1952 onwards the debt would continuously increase (see table 33). During Velasco's presidency, Ecuador's internal public debt escalated by a factor of 287.6%. Likewise, Ecuador's foreign debts, the total of both private and public, continued to increase after 1952 (see table 34).

[156] *Indices económicos del Ecuador. Country Statistics.*

[157] United States of America. Department of State. Office of the Historian. *Memorandum of a Conversation, Department of State, Washington, August 31, 1955.* Accessed July 17, 2011. http://history.state.gov/historicaldocuments/frus1955-57v07/d471.

Table 33: Ecuador internal public debt, 1948-1972[158]

Year	Total Debt (millions of sucres)	Year	Total Debt (millions of sucres)
1948	112	1961	1,927
1949	111	1962	2,213
1950	126	1963	2,577
1951	105	1964	3,077
1952	121	1965	3,474
1953	186	1966	4,403
1954	189	1967	4,494
1955	232	1968	5,376
1956	469	1969	7,747
1957	470	1970	7,908
1958	507	1971	8,152
1959	707	1972	8,962
1960	1,196		

Table 34: Ecuador external debt, 1950-1972[159]

Year	Total Debt (millions of USD)	Year	Total Debt (millions of USD)
1950	26.1	1962	93.0
1951	24.5	1963	102.7
1952	25.2	1964	103.2
1953	28.9	1965	110.0
1954	29.0	1966	121.3
1955	39.0	1967	140.7
1956	48.1	1968	163.3
1957	61.6	1969	196.2
1958	64.2	1970	213.1
1959	63.0	1971	241.5
1960	68.3	1972	260.8
1961	83.4		

Within this context, protests against the government began to escalate, and student and labor manifestations were repressed with violence. Similarly, several critical media outlets, like *El Universo* newspaper in Guayaquil due to the critical writings of Alejandro Carrión (also famous with his pen name *Juan Sin Cielo* and who later wrote for *El Comercio*),

---

158 *Indices económicos del Ecuador. Country Statistics.*

159 *Indices económicos del Ecuador. Country Statistics.*

were also subjugated. Opposing political parties were also pressured by the central government. This tense sociopolitical climate got even worse when Velasco's Minister of Government, Camilo Ponce Enriquez, resigned in order to run for the presidency in the 1956 elections.

Ponce Enriquez' main adversary in the race for the presidency was Raul Clemente Huerta and his vice-presidential candidate José María Plaza, the former president's brother. From the beginning, the political contest was a heated one. Backed by Velasco, Ponce Enriquez' political party, the *Alianza Popular*, would benefit from the sitting president's genius populist rhetoric. His words would again go down in history when in reference to Huerta-Plaza's *Frente Democrático* party, he famously declared "O el Frente me tritura a mi, o yo trituro al Frente" (Either *el Frente* triturates me, or I'll triturate *el Frente*). As votes were counted and recounted, the Supreme Electoral Tribunal would declare Camilo Ponce the winner over Raul Clemente Huerta with a skintight margin of 178,424 votes to 175,378.

The close victory margin and annulments of several electoral parishes exacerbated the numerous accusations of electoral fraud present during the electoral process. This condition fueled an uprising in Manabí, headed by the Frente Democrático, to contest the suspiciously elected frontrunner. True to his threat, Velasco sent troops to quell this unrest, which was believed to be organizing out of the hacienda of former Galo Plaza governor, Homero Andrade Alcívar. An aerial firing squad was sent to Andrade's estate near the city of Chone, and followed through with forceful actions in the rest of the country. He succeeded. The rebellion was aborted, and Camilo Ponce Enriquez assumed the presidency on September 1, 1956.

Just like Plaza and Velasco, Camilo Ponce would successfully complete his presidential term. Not since the cacao era had three presidents completed full back-to-back presidential terms. The prosperity brought in by the banana bonanza assured 12 years of relative political stability. Even with consideration of Velasco's spending habits, the healthiness of the economy assured Ponce would not have to deal with a liquidated government and even received a letter from U.S. President Eisenhower in April 1958 in which the North American described Ecuador as "a nation enjoying political stability, freedom and steady economic development."[160] The government nevertheless increased internal public debt by 155% during the four years of Camilo Ponce's presidency. Further in 1957, as the banana industry significantly decreased in its growth rate, which had grown at a rate of 25% a year from 1950 to 1955, but only 12% a year from 1955 to 1960, the Ponce government requested a $15 million loan for infrastructure projects.[161] With no imminent need to cut back spending, and with the circumstance of a still wholesome economy, the Ponce administration would continue to increase government expenditure.

Works like a bridge over the Guayas River, the development of seaports in San Lorenzo, Bahía de Caraquez, Puerto Bolívar, and most significantly the renovated seaport in Guayaquil, were all projects carried through during Ponce's presidency. Even more, motivated by the Eleventh Pan-American Conference that was to be held in Quito in 1960, government funds, as well as a $2.5 million loan from Eximbank, were used to improve the nation's capital with a new legislative palace, justice building, a building for the comptroller general, a building for the social security administration, the International Hotel in Quito, among others, including the Mariscal Sucre International Airport. This rate of government spending could not withstand a debilitating economy. In 1959, three years into Ponce's presidency, a depleted economy resulted in vandalisms and looting of several commercial stores. Aggressions towards innocent by-standers who where robbed at all hours of the day also became frequent. This lawlessness in turn, resulted in the bloody 1959 repression of May 9th in Portoviejo, and of June 3rd in Guayaquil, where dozens of criminals were apprehended but not without innocent civilian casualties.[162]

Still, Ponce would complete his four-year term. But before he would bestow the presidential band on the new president, he would foresee a relatively quiet 1960 presidential campaign between frontrunners Galo Plaza and Gonzalo Cordero Crespo. That is, until José María Velasco Ibarra, like a "role to the fore," ran for president yet again. Slamming his

---

[160] United States of America. Department of State. Office of the Historian. *Editorial Note.* Vol. V. Series 306. Department of State. Accessed July 17, 2011. http://history.state.gov/historicaldocuments/frus1958-60v05/d306.

[161] Pineo, *Useful Strangers,* 1843.

[162] Dobronski, *El Ecuador: Los hechos más importantes de su historia,* 328.

opponents and promising a "land of milk and honey,"[163] Velasco was elected with what Assistant Secretary of State for Inter-American Affairs Roy Rubottom would term "a surprisingly large margin."[164] He then assumed, for an unprecedented fourth time, the presidency of the Republic of Ecuador on September 1, 1960.

Velasco would swiftly and characteristically begin spending and increasing bureaucracy with fellow loyalists. This time however, unlike his third presidency 8 years earlier, Velasco was confronted with a waning banana economy and could do little to fulfill the promises he had made to the Ecuadorian people. Land reform and tax breaks for the deprived were simply not going to happen. An incredibly astute politician as he was, he would divert attention to the nation's foreign policy agenda. Consequently, shortly thereafter, students demonstrating over the boundary dispute with Peru stoned the consulate of that nation and the consulate general of the United States in Guayaquil.[165] The following month, on October 23 1960, Velasco Ibarra would appeal to the patriotic sentiments of the Ecuadorian people, and declare the 1942 Rio Protocol to be null and void.

The renunciation of the 1942 Protocol built on top of what during the Plaza government had been declared the unenforceability of the document, and on top of the opinions of national and international jurists who had concluded the unjust nature of the document.[166] Nevertheless, Velasco's hold on power would start to dwindle when he agreed to raise taxes in order to secure a loan from the International Monetary Fund. As expected, this decision was extremely unpopular and resulted in most of the nation opposing the president. Symptomatically, Velasco would respond with violent repression, arresting members of the opposition, repressing the media, and even hiring thugs to beat opponents.[167]

---

[163] Pineo, *Useful Strangers*, 1878.

[164] United States of America. Department of State. Office of the Historian. *Editorial Note*. Vol. V. Series 306.

[165] United States of America. Department of State. Office of the Historian. *Editorial Note*. Vol. V. Series 306.

[166] Dobronski, *El Ecuador: Los hechos más importantes de su historia*, 330.

[167] Pineo, *Useful Strangers*, 1913.

Things really became chaotic when citizens stormed into congress and started throwing stones and rotten fruit at legislators, forcing them to seek cover under their desks. If that was not enough, disputing congressmen resorted to opening gunfire on each other. Principally among the performers of the gunfight was Velasco's vice-president, Carlos Julio Arosemena Monroy, who was serving as head of congress and who had been building support and distancing himself from Velasco. He famously spoke about "men maddened by money," a reference surely to Velasco's decision to raise taxes and accept the IMF loan. Following this, on November 3, 1961, Velasco decided to solemnize with his presence a student protest in the city of Cuenca, which eventually escalated into the falling-out of the nation's two foremost judges.[168] Velasco then had Arosemena arrested claiming the vice-president was attempting to seize power away from him and make himself dictator.

Subsequently, on November 7, 1961, a day after the arrest of the vice-president, the army decided to rid Velasco and vice-president Arosemena from power. The air force, however, accompanied with the pressure of public opinion, would disagree and vowed to start bombing runs against the army if they did not support the vice-president in assuming the position of head of state. The army yielded, and congress elected Carlos Julio Arosemena Monroy as president of Ecuador. Velasco's fourth presidency had lasted fourteen months. He sought asylum in the Mexican embassy, and shortly afterwards, at the same time Arosemena was arriving at the Carondelet Palace as president, he fled for Mexico vowing to return.[167]

Arosemena's presidency began in favorable political circumstances. All the major political factions supported the new head of state; and even his notorious indulgences of "masculine vices" (alcohol), which resulted in several infamous stories,[169] were overlooked. It was not until the internal quarrels over how to stand towards Cuba (the Church wanted nothing to do with a communist nation, as did the military), which had been forcefully influenced by the United States, that things began to affect

---

168 Dobronski, *El Ecuador: Los hechos más importantes de su historia*, 329.

169 Among the folk stories related with Arosemena's alcohol use is his urinating on a plant in the middle of a conference being held at a Quito Hotel. Also, after drunkenly exiting a helicopter in the typically summer-dry province of Manabí, he proclaimed his happiness to find Manabí so green after observing the landscape through green shade glasses.

the Arosemena presidency. During this time, the Banana trade continued to dwindle, and Velasco's spending habits had affected the central government's position. This irresponsible spending resulted in what Ecuadorian ambassador to the United States José Chiriboga Villagómez termed as the "economic dictatorship." This term alluded to the fact that the United States had held back loans to Ecuador because it did not take a more hostile stance towards communist Cuba.[170]

On top of the quarrels over what position to take towards Cuba, a despicable and very public act of corruption publicly unfolded in which high-ranking functionaries of the Velasco regime had purchased junk military equipment. Intra-government clashes and cases of corruption (even though these had mainly been carried out during Velasco's presidency) were accompanied by a troubled economy, which from 1961 to 1963 resulted in a decrease of government expenditure, an increase in debt, and a decrease in per capita GDP from 1962 to 1963. Perhaps stemming from the decline in the price of banana, which from 1960 to 1962 decreased by 7.7%, finances would hurt during the Arosemena presidency. The economy would not experience a breather until 1963, year when news that Velasco Ibarra would return as candidate for the 1964 election, encouraged the military to take a hold on power.

As power was taken from unpredictable Arosemena, the customary practice of the military of entrusting the presidency to a civilian never happened. And just as they would do during the onset of Ecuador's third commodity boom, the military themselves decided to govern the country just as the economy received good news, banana prices were up 26.7% from 1962 to 1963 and production was increasing. The context in which the military junta assumed power in 1963, allowed them to execute their plan, and ever did they have one (a 21-volume, 3000-page document titled *Plan General de Desarrollo Económico y Social 1963*-1973). The junta, headed by Rear Admiral Castro Jijón, would govern with astonishing contradictions. While they would repudiate communism, they insisted on directing a planned economy with emphasis on industrialization. Though they maintained at repressing labor, they vowed to carry out land reform. Lamentably, though perhaps not unexpectedly, the military junta's government failed miserably, especially at their signature project of agrarian reorganization.

---

[170] Pineo, *Useful Strangers*, 2060.

Land reform began in the most obvious of properties, the famously immense Hacienda Tenguel. The United Fruit Company had endured difficulties in Tenguel with the neighboring Mollepongo Comune; a court battle loss against the Colonia Agrícola Shumiral in 1960; and finally the workers' invasion of the hacienda in 1962. In 1963, as part of the larger goal of distributing land throughout the entire nation, a military base was permanently established at the former United Fruit administration building to assure reform in the property.[171] The state's agrarian reform institute, the IERAC, was created and filled with a monstrous bureaucratic contraption in order to oversee the implementation of land restructuring.

Thousands of extremely fertile hectares of farmland were appropriated at Tenguel and other properties and given to ex-workers. By 1966, agrarian reform had resulted in a complete and utter failure. After restructuring, 73.1% of the population held 7.1% of the land, while 0.4% of the population held 45.1% of the nation's farmland. Moreover, banana production took a dive after 1963 with exports decreasing from 1,014,340 metric tons to 874,580 in two years, signifying a decrease of 26.3% in export revenue. In the end, reform resulted in the emergence of contract farming and in a new class of an agrarian bourgeoisie that developed as a result of ex-worker peasants selling their land to new capitalists that in turn resulted in ex-worker peasants becoming workers again. In haciendas like Tenguel, workers were dispossessed through agrarian reform, a bizarre process that integrated the betrayal of state officials, the trickery of local capitalists, and the complicity of military forces.[172]

In the three years of the military junta's government, efforts were made to enact productive reform. Agrarian restructuring became a mess, yet smaller projects like the *Ley de Cheques*, a law evocative of the Edwin Kemmerer recommendations, attended to a widely problematic situation of extensive check fraud and abuse. Nevertheless, after 1964, the banana export economy was in a state of crisis and the junta would struggle to hold favorable public opinion. Small-scale banana producers suffered widely as a result of a decrease in the price per stem, which tumbled from twenty-three sucres to eight. Government debt continued to increase in order to finance the government's current expenditure, which had increased 17% in a year, and which would result in a 1,000,000,000 sucres

---

[171] Striffler, *In the Shadows of State and Capital*, 130.

[172] Striffler, *In the Shadows of State and Capital*, 129.

(an alarming amount at the time) budget deficit in 1966. And perhaps more troubling, the cost of living had increased over 15% with real wages increasing only 1.5%.[173] Like this, the military government stepped down in March, 1966 after alienating nearly every sector of the Ecuadorian people. It entrusted Clemente Yerovi as interim president, who would govern for eight months.

Stabilization and the End of the Banana Economy

Otto Arosemena Gómez (cousin of former president Carlos Julio Arosemena Monroy) rose to the presidency of Ecuador as the interim president of the 1966 constituent assembly on November 16. He was seen as business friendly and able to direct the country out of the crisis. The national deficit had been somewhat cured in the eight months after the military had stepped down, although it was still considered the most important issue to be addressed. As such, the new president proclaimed on the 29th of November, "The first and most critical of problems that need to be addressed is that of fiscal order."[174] To this point, the government prepared a budget law that aimed at controlling unnecessary government spending. His choices of collaborators seem to have been spot-on, and among others, included Homero Andrade Alcívar as Minister of Agriculture, and Benjamin Terán Varea as Minister of Government.

The government began with an optimistic political climate propelled by the expectations generated by the new constitution. Additionally, Ecuador's most important export experienced an upturn from 1966 onwards, increasing production by 17.6% during Arosemena's two-year term. This increase in production also boosted banana export revenue by 55.3% in the same timespan even when international banana prices experienced little change. Everyday problems, such as the milk crisis, in which producers were hampered by a price ceiling established by the previous administration, was swiftly lifted by Arosemena's progressive Minister of Agriculture.

Government income, which had decreased from 1965 to 1966, increased during Otto Arosemena's presidency. Likewise, government

---

[173] Blasco Peñaherrera, *Historia Del Ecuador,* edited by Ricardo Martín (Barcelona: Salvat Editores, 1980).

[174] "Problemas Fiscales Y Laborales Afronta El Gobierno Interino," *El Tiempo* (Quito), November 30, 1966.

expenditure also increased together with increased internal and external debt, of which the latter increased by an average of 14.9% a year; 12.6% a year until 1972. This time however, the steep increase in debt was accompanied by an event that would change Ecuadorian history forever. As it happened, on March 29, 1967, the Texaco-Gulf consortium, which had signed a concession agreement with the government in 1964, struck oil at Lago Agrio deposit number 1. Drillers had tapped into what turned out to be a massive underground sea of petroleum. This fact quickly changed the international outlook on Ecuador and the country began encountering fewer obstacles when requesting financing.

The prospect of oil started a period of intense debt accumulation, which began with the financing of a 504-kilometer pipeline that would travel from the province of Sucumbios in the Ecuadorian orient, over the Andes, and to San Lorenzo in the Ecuadorian north coast onto the port of Balao. The pipeline would be completed in 1972 at a cost of $130 million.[175] Otto Arosemena's two-year presidential term would end with only his provocative foreign policy stances, such as his outspoken participation at the inter-American presidential meeting in Punta del Este, as occurrences for reflection.

With bananas still in their positive stride, and with the prospect of oil opulence ahead, Velasco Ibarra and his famous populist discourse overcame a variety of opponents to win the 1968 presidential election. His fifth and final term in office would differ little from his previous mandates. His campaign promises, which aroused Ecuadorians with unrealistic expectations, were abandoned. Instead, he tried to correct the characteristic superfluous spending of his previous administrations and, perhaps due to the fact that the president was now limited by the new constitution in his abilities to handle money at his discretion, adopted a policy of austerity.

In 1969, schoolteachers and government employees went on strike. Additionally that year, exports decreased by 14%. In order to increase government funds, Velasco began to aggressively tax the country; he eliminated tax incentives on industry, increased the sales tax, and even taxed public works projects. By April 1970, students were holding daily protests on the streets, and the results of regional elections proved disastrous for the government. Henceforth, on June 22 he decided to

---

[175] Pineo, *Useful Strangers*, 2145.

assume all powers and declare himself dictator. He rapidly seized congress and closed down universities, but the unrest intensified. The chaos that unfolded for the next 21 months finally resulted in the military deciding they were the only ones that could restore order. Conveniently, the military arrived at this conclusion just as the oil pipeline was to begin operations. José María Velasco Ibarra was removed from his fifth presidential post and left for Argentina, where he would stay until 1979, year in which he would return to Ecuador to, as he put it, "meditate and die."

The banana bonanza, spearheaded by United Fruit's operations, saw Ecuador enjoy political stability. The vast influx of capital spread throughout the country, many entrepreneurs benefitted from a burgeoning business environment, and the government had healthy coffers that allowed it to manage the nation even when destructive earthquakes shattered the cities of Latacunga and Ambato. Healthy finances and GDP growth resulted in a content citizenry as well as stable governments that produced effective diplomatic efforts. This period contrasts sharply with the continuous political crises that occurred from 1925 through 1948. It was only after the banana economy began to slow down that Ecuador's events would resemble those of the age of crises when governments would topple and constitutional order be ruined.

The years from 1948 to 1972 represented a period of rapid growth for Ecuador. The banana explosion generated wealth for many Ecuadorians, but even with government incentives aimed at using the banana boom to industrialize the nation, Ecuador struggled in this regard. While in Latin America, the average contribution of industry to GDP expanded from 17% in 1940 to 25% in 1970, in Ecuador the change was from 16% to 17% during the same time.[176] Although it should also be noted that U.S. aid to Ecuador frequently lagged behind what other nations were receiving. In point of fact, from 1945 to 1957 the United States completed $2.6 billion in grants and credit to Latin America with Ecuador receiving only 2%.[177] Moreover, of all the Eximbank loans to the region, Ecuador would receive only about 0.6%.[178]

---

[176] Pineo, *Useful Strangers*, 1654.

[177] Pineo, *Useful Strangers*, 1823.

[178] Pineo, *Useful Strangers*, 1852.

Ecuadorian exports would dramatically increase by an average of 7.9% per year between 1948 and 1972 (see table 35). This increase in commerce resulted in increased population, with much of the rural population relocating to the cities. The population of Quito went from about 150,00 in 1947 to 700,000 inhabitants in 1974. Likewise, Guayaquil would grow from a city of 180,000 people to a metropolis of close to one million. The coastal city would increase at a faster rate given the banana-industry-propelled migration of many Ecuadorians to the coast. Overall, the population of Ecuador expanded at an average of 2.8% a year (see table 36), one of the highest growth rates in the world at the time. GDP grew at an annual rate of over 5%, and per capita GDP at an annual rate of 2%. The banana-fueled economy, though more powerful than the cacao era in its effect on the country, would pale in comparison to the influence Ecuador's third commodity boom would have.

Table 35: Total country exports, 1948-1972[179]

Year	Exports in USD x 1000	Year	Exports in USD x 1000
1948	49,025	1961	96,647
1949	31,378	1962	116,917
1950	64,243	1963	131,215
1951	52,160	1964	130,364
1952	76,702	1965	133,790
1953	72,698	1966	147,499
1954	100,219	1967	166,036
1955	89,861	1968	176,559
1956	94,430	1969	151,886
1957	98,636	1970	189,929
1958	96,382	1971	199,075
1959	97,245	1972	326,292
1960	102,561		

[179] *Indices económicos del Ecuador. Country Statistics.*

Table 36: Population of ecuador 1948-1972[180]

Year	Population	Year	Population
1948	3,270,403	1961	4,569,675
1949	3,328,649	1962	4,705,884
1950	3,387,358	1963	4,847,182
1951	3,475,951	1964	4,993,359
1952	3,567,080	1965	5,144,208
1953	3,661,402	1966	5,299,868
1954	3,759,571	1967	5,460,478
1955	3,862,242	1968	5,625,829
1956	3,968,978	1969	5,795,712
1957	4,079,343	1970	5,969,918
1958	4,193,992	1971	6,148,361
1959	4,313,580	1972	6,331,179
1960	4,438,761		

[180] *Indices económicos del Ecuador. Country Statistics.*

Picture 15: President Galo Plaza Lasso

Picture 16: Map showing the different topography than the one described on the 1941 Rio Protocol

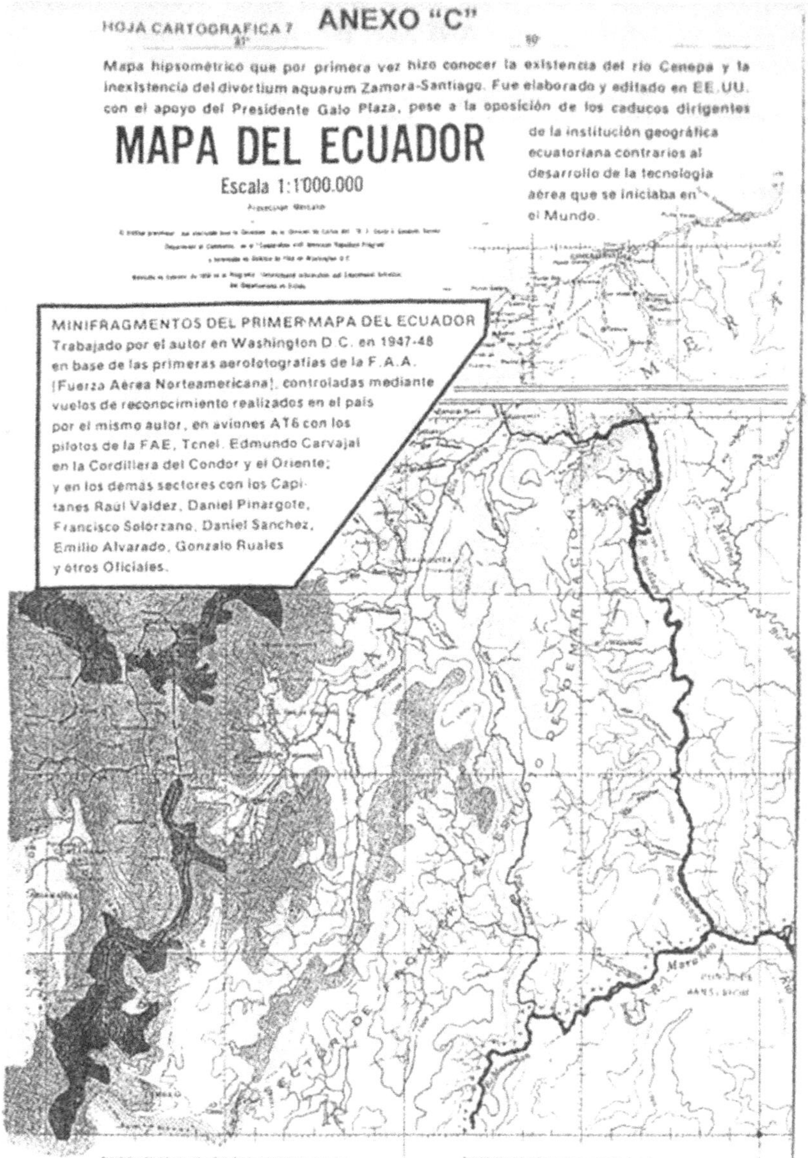

Picture 17: Velasco Ibarra declaring the nullity of the 1941 Rio Protocol in Riobamba

El Protocolo de Río es nulo y jamás lo reconoceremos, dice el Dr. Velasco Ibarra

Ecuador exige que se reconozca su derecho a tener un puerto en el Amazonas y un asiento en Oriente, base de la nacionalidad, expr

Asistió a solemne inauguración de monumento al héroe nacional Cap. E. Chiriboga

Picture 18: President Velasco Ibarra aboard a military aircraft

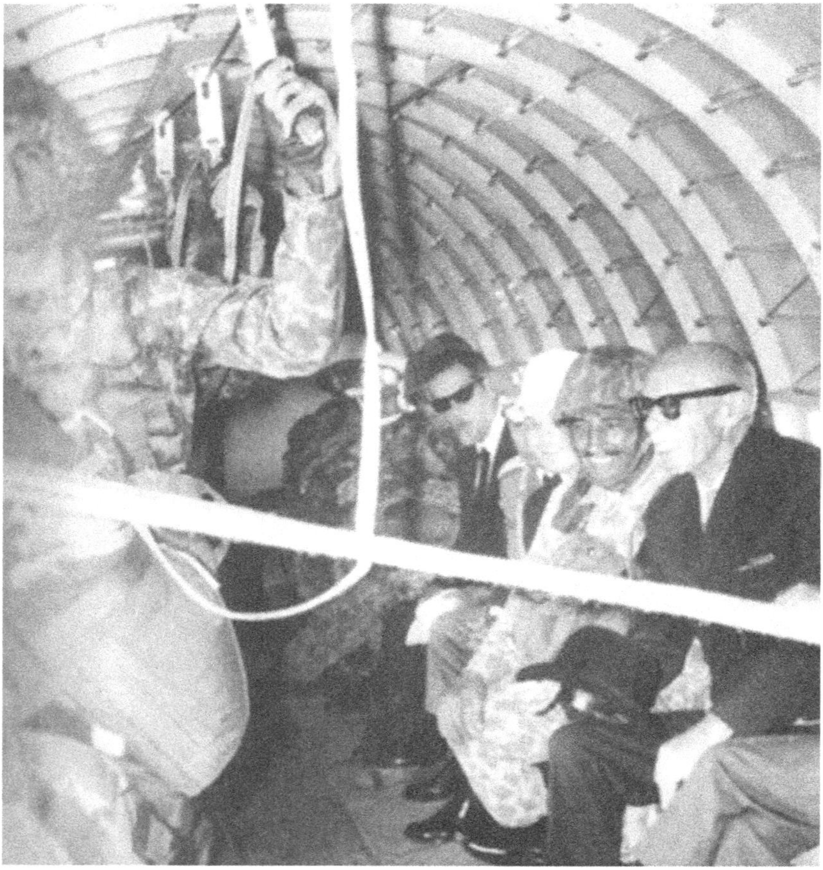

Picture 19: Homero Andrade Alcívar & Galo Plaza Lasso

Chapter 4

Oil, Riches, Debts & Crises (1972-2000)

The final quarter century in Ecuador would unfold just as the other three; stability would be in striking correlation with economic performance, and this time, economic performance would be entwined with the behavior of what would become Ecuador's third commodity boom in a century. A commodity boom indeed, Ecuador would change at a rate not seen since the Spanish colonization of the continent 5 centuries earlier. All demographic and economic indicators would significantly change beginning in 1972; technology, consumer culture, politics, war, trade, debt, everything would be affected by petroleum.

Used since ancient times,[181] Ecuadorians have known the utility of oil for centuries. Even before the Spanish disembarked on the Americas, natives would use the black sticky substance to seal canoes and make torches. Pre-Colombian societies, and later the Spanish, would dig pits that would fill with oil, and in time the pools would evaporate into tar, the product that was used to stick boats together and light paths at night. Back then, however, oil was not as important to everyday life and the economy as it has become in the 20th and 21st centuries. In Ecuador, most of this oil came from pits dug in the Santa Elena peninsula. In point of fact, the first oil well in Ecuador was constructed there in the early 20th century. Output, nevertheless, was low and so exploration was directed towards the Ecuadorian orient when Standard Oil was granted a concession to explore the area in 1921.

Decades passed and no petroleum was found in the Ecuadorian Amazon. The long and unfruitful quest even led Ecuadorian president Galo Plaza Lasso to declare that the oriente is a myth,[182] that there was simply no oil in the Ecuadorian orient. Plaza, however, was proven wrong almost two decades later when in 1967, the Texaco-Gulf consortium

---

[181] Oil from pits was used to build walls and towers in ancient Babylonia.

[182] Allen Gerlach, *Indians, Oil, and Politics: A Recent History of Ecuador* (Wilmington, DE: Scholarly Resources, 2003), 33.

discovered an underground sea of petroleum in the Sucumbios province on northeastern Ecuador. By 1972, a 500km Trans-Ecuadorian Pipe Line (SOTE), which was privately built and which was to be privately operated for twenty-five years, started producing 250,000 barrels per day.[182] This number would increase throughout the rest of the 20th century, yet Ecuador would never produce over 0.5% of the world's crude. Nonetheless, the country would still rely on its revenue for about half of government income.

Black Gold: Oil Explodes in Ecuador

When oil started flowing through SOTE in 1972, the 500km pipeline that rose 4,000 meters over the Andes to reach the ports of Ecuador's pacific cost, the price per barrel for the country's crude stood at $2.50. This price and output meant that Ecuador began exporting an extra $59,452,000 almost overnight (see table 37, 38). Furthermore, this meant that oil and its derivatives reached a level of 18.4% of all country exports in the first six months of production. The following year, prices came close to doubling at $4.20, and export revenue that year is not shy in showing this. The increase in price continued in 1974 when Ecuadorian crude reached a price of $13.70, an increase of over 226%. By 1980, Ecuadorian crude stood at over $35. During the 1970s, oil earnings catapulted each year over the previous one transforming Ecuador with analogous bounds.

Table 37: Oil exports, 1972-2000[183]

Year	Amount in US dollars (FOB) x 1000	Year	Amount in US dollars (FOB) x 1000
1972	59,452	1987	647,273
1973	282,057	1988	875,174
1974	692,769	1989	1,032,698
1975	587,118	1990	1,268,151
1976	739,290	1991	1,058,594
1977	702,280	1992	1,259,596
1978	622,555	1993	1,152,144
1979	1,036,212	1994	1,185,033
1980	1,393,927	1995	1,395,480
1981	1,559,061	1996	1,520,815
1982	1,390,178	1997	1,411,577
1983	1,551,535	1998	788,974
1984	1,678,237	1999	1,312,311
1985	1,824,662	2000	2,144,009
1986	912,395		

Unlike the previous commodity booms in Ecuador, the petroleum bang occurred beyond the country's coast and did not suffer from the variables of weather and disease like cacao or bananas. The oil was located in the Ecuadorian orient, far away from any urban center and its main performance variable was its quotation from the international markets (see table 38). Also unlike previous commodity surges, oil was not managed by farmers or industrialists, but rather by the central government, meaning that for the first time in Ecuadorian history the government had its own source of income. Accordingly, revenue generated by oil went directly into government coffers. This newfound wealth financed spending unprecedented in the nation's history, and altogether changed the face of the country. In the decade following 1972, public expenditure increased at an annual rate of 12% and rose from 22% to 33% of GDP. Oil resulted in a surge of foreign exchange earnings, increasing by a factor of eight in just three years following 1971, and almost instantly provided nearly one-half of all government income.[184]

---

[183] *Indices económicos del Ecuador. Country Statistics.*

[184] Gerlach. *Indians, Oil, and Politics*, 33.

Table 38: WTI oil prices per barrel 1972-2000[185]

Year	Average Period Price	Real price (2012)	Year	Average Period Price	Real price (2012)
1972	3.45	18.92	1987	19.16	38.63
1973	4.51	23.27	1988	15.98	30.95
1974	12.28	57.05	1989	19.61	36.23
1975	12.67	53.97	1990	24.51	42.97
1976	13.32	53.63	1991	21.55	36.25
1977	14.22	53.75	1992	20.57	33.59
1978	14.85	52.18	1993	18.46	29.26
1979	25.10	79.22	1994	17.21	26.60
1980	37.89	105.34	1995	18.41	27.68
1981	36.15	91.10	1996	22.13	32.31
1982	32.65	77.51	1997	20.60	29.41
1983	30.62	70.43	1998	14.43	20.28
1984	29.41	64.84	1999	19.32	26.56
1985	27.93	59.47	2000	30.38	40.41
1986	15.04	31.45			

The state quickly became the center of the economy and Quito became the political and financial hub of the country. Buildings were erected and the capital's streets became congested with the ever-growing number of automobiles. Economic growth expanded the middle class while people from the provinces migrated to the large urban centers as the economy ceased being predominantly agricultural. Population grew exponentially in the capital as the economy was transformed into one where services, industry, manufacturing, and mining played ever-increasing roles. Quito transformed from a city of 565,000 people in 1970, into a metropolis of 1.1 million in 1982 (see table 39), while the entire population of the country grew 32.8% from 1972 to 1982 (see table 40).

[185] "West Texas Intermediate Oil Price (US$/Barrel)," Global Financial Data. Accessed August 17, 2012. http://www.globalfinancialdata.com/.

Table 39: Population of Quito, 1972-2001[186]

Year	Population x 1000 (metropolitan area)	Year	Population x 1000 (metropolitan area)
1970	528.1 (565.0)	1989	1234.0
1974	599.8 (636.0)	1990	1100.8
1982	890.4 (1110.2)	1995	1401.4
1983	918.9	1996	1444.4
1986	1093.0	2001	1399.8
1987	1138.0		

Table 40: Population of Ecuador, 1972-2001[187]

Year	Population	Year	Population
1972	6,331,179	1987	9,561,489
1973	6,518,503	1988	9,804,403
1974	6,710,462	1989	10,039,775
1975	6,907,185	1990	10,271,874
1976	7,109,212	1991	10,503,491
1977	7,316,456	1992	10,735,969
1978	7,528,109	1993	10,965,121
1979	7,743,360	1994	11,186,758
1980	7,961,402	1995	11,396,692
1981	8,183,120	1996	11,591,131
1982	8,409,053	1997	11,772,866
1983	8,637,873	1998	11,947,588
1984	8,868,249	1999	12,120,984
1985	9,098,852	2000	12,298,745
1986	9,329,636	2001	12,479,924

The country's dependence on the spectacularly performing commodity assured that taxes remained low for most citizens and even experienced a relative decrease towards the end of the 1970s. Needless to say, Ecuadorians quickly became accustomed to development and prosperity. Imports radically increased after 1972 at an average rate of 24.43% per year towards 1980, even when import taxes increased. A consumer culture also rapidly developed and the result was a swift increase in the importation of consumer goods, which increased at a rate of 21.11% per year during the same period (see table 41). Moreover, all petroleum-related products were heavily subsidized by the central

186 Jan Lahmeyer, "Ecuador: Urban Population."

187 *Indices económicos del Ecuador. Country Statistics.*

government, which meant that Ecuadorians became accustomed to cheap gasoline and low-priced natural gas used for cooking, which by century's end attained a cost of about $5 to produce but sold for only $1.

Table 41: Imports destinations in thousands of U.S. dollars (CIF), 1972-2000[188]

Year	Total	Consumer goods	Fuels & lubricants	Source materials	Capital goods	Other
1972	318,599	46,228	10,602	135,042	125,687	1,040
1973	397,282	64,064	11,183	173,829	147,856	350
1974	958,488	116,076	16,284	435,295	388,570	2,263
1975	943,244	102,576	13,575	375,260	448,295	3,538
1976	993,123	99,178	7,419	445,805	438,294	2,427
1977	1,508,357	167,817	9,375	602,796	724,435	3,934
1978	1,630,202	178,550	11,099	609,697	826,933	3,923
1979	1,985,599	180,481	13,541	831,319	955,343	4,915
1980	2,249,519	250,171	23,281	942,978	1,016,705	16,384
1981	2,246,162	202,722	25,752	922,676	1,085,516	9,496
1982	1,988,374	224,820	26,479	917,310	815,733	4,032
1983	1,464,954	183,710	19,263	843,393	402,782	15,806
1984	1,715,777	143,162	21,727	960,700	588,331	1,857
1985	1,766,724	152,486	198,304	890,411	525,524	0
1986	1,810,224	169,610	113,384	851,239	672,127	3,864
1987	2,158,136	208,401	294,500	917,928	732,019	5,289
1988	1,713,525	164,565	58,733	820,929	665,772	3,526
1989	1,854,781	184,361	71,101	981,746	608,546	9,027
1990	1,865,126	177,856	94,627	979,466	609,324	3,853
1991	2,399,040	248,522	91,685	1,169,939	887,602	1,292
1992	2,430,978	385,438	101,238	1,024,918	917,008	2,377
1993	2,562,223	542,105	87,634	946,261	984,270	1,953
1994	3,622,019	809,905	103,823	1,317,668	1,390,088	535
1995	4,152,635	823,189	240,886	1,709,161	1,378,174	1,225
1996	3,931,720	856,568	162,368	1,758,673	1,153,048	1,063
1997	4,954,834	1,039,660	437,434	1,996,345	1,480,540	854
1998	5,575,734	1,170,817	325,578	2,205,047	1,873,511	781
1999	3,017,256	621,168	243,838	1,335,475	815,058	1,715
2000	3,721,201	821,386	298,204	1,657,764	941,847	2,000

Within this context, the government led by General Guillermo Rodriguez Lara (1972-1976), also known as "Bombita," assumed the control of the

[188] *Indices económicos del Ecuador. Country Statistics.*

Republic. A member of the Ecuadorian military leadership, Rodriguez Lara assumed power after deposing civilian dictator Velasco Ibarra, and just a few short months prior to the 1972 onset of oil opulence. It cannot be ascertained whether the ousting of Velasco was intended to coincide with the start of petroleum flowing through the country, but it cannot be denied that it secured the new military government's hold on power. The amount of income and spending occurring during the 1970s was without precedent in Ecuadorian history, and the citizenry at large made no apologies in accepting the privileges produced by the production of petroleum.

Unlike other military dictatorships in Latin America at the time, the officers ruling Ecuador went without the atrocious methods of terror that were being used elsewhere. In Ecuador, the government did not have the need to control the "unruly" popular classes and instead used their dictatorial powers and newfound wealth to install social reform that would, as the government proclaimed, "help the underprivileged and take Ecuador to join the ranks of modernized nations." This program became known as *revolutionary nationalism*, and was indeed felt across the country due to the amount of money that was being disbursed throughout Ecuador. From the beginning, Rodriguez Lara used all resources to secure income, credit, and swift spending.

The first order of business of the new government was to secure a larger share of petroleum revenue for the state. The heightened expectations created by the military government's nationalistic speech, obligated a renegotiation of petroleum contracts in 1972. And as prices rose sharply during the decade, so did state income, which by 1980 reached levels many times higher than before. Revenue became five times more than what Velasco Ibarra's regime took in, and twenty times as much as the government of Galo Plaza Lasso's.[189] In point of fact, state revenue would increase by almost a factor of four in the first three years of oil production alone, and 6.4 times by the time the military would step down as heads of government in 1979 (see table 42).

---

[189] Gerlach, *Indians, Oil, and Politics*, 36.

Table 42: Government income in millions of U.S. dollars, 1972-2000[190]

Year	Total Income	% Of GNP	Income from Oil	Non-oil Income
1972	288.6	14.9	36.1	230.4
1973	494.6	19.1	135.6	309.0
1974	945.2	24.1	401.8	396.4
1975	1,088.0	23.4	382.0	448.6
1976	1,157.0	20.4	401.3	530.4
1977	1,331.5	19.2	407.0	649.8
1978	1,535.3	21.2	458.6	769.7
1979	1,854.6	20.1	678.7	879.6
1980	2,220.6	20.3	786.0	921.5
1981	2,404.1	19.2	815.7	1,014.4
1982	2,222.1	18.5	898.4	878.2
1983	1,243.8	18.4	549.9	471.7
1984	1,649.5	19.0	694.5	693.2
1985	2,820.2	24.6	1,435.0	1,021.5
1986	2,216.7	20.2	728.7	1,121.4
1987	1,986.3	19.7	581.7	1,006.3
1988	1,842.4	18.9	605.3	937.0
1989	2,024.1	21.6	830.2	906.3
1990	2,275.0	22.0	1,024.3	910.5
1991	2,334.5	20.5	951.7	1,035.6
1992	2,584.8	21.8	1,133.3	1,063.7
1993	2,863.0	20.0	1,189.2	1,213.8
1994	3,213.6	17.6	1,190.9	1,506.0
1995	3,865.8	19.3	1,323.2	1,723.8
1996	3,730.2	17.5	1,674.3	1,579.1
1997	3,651.0	15.4	1,236.4	2,042.8
1998	3,393.0	14.6	909.2	2,100.8
1999	2,934.9	18.0	1,048.0	1,583.6
2000	3,412.1	21.4	1,313.3	1,870.9

Increased state revenue resulted in a stronger central government, which in turn produced the aggressive takeover of an ever-growing government conglomerate that was funded through significant state ownership of the oil industry, and with taxes levied on foreign oil companies. During the 1970s and into the 1980s, the Ecuadorian government gradually took over the Texaco Gulf consortium, as well as other enterprises. In 1972, the Ecuadorian State Petroleum Corporation

[190] *Indices económicos del Ecuador. Country Statistics.*

(CEPE), which was formed during Velasco Ibarra's last presidential term, revised the terms under which foreign companies could operate in Ecuador, and put in place new retroactive taxes; increased state royalties on exports; and renegotiated all land concessions, which by 1973 had returned 5.63 million hectares of oil land back to Ecuador. Furthermore, CEPE acquired 25% of Texaco-Gulf, only to increase its share to 51% shortly afterwards. In 1976, CEPE expanded its takeover of Ecuadorian oil operations by taking over Anglo Ecuadorian Oil Field Ltd. But perhaps most significant was Ecuador's expansion into petroleum refinement with investment in the Esmeraldas oil refinery that went into operation in 1977. Government expenditure was increasing at a rate analogous to state income, growing at a 25.1% average per year (income grew at an average rate of 25.5% per year) from 1972 to 1980 (see table 43).

Table 43: Government Expenditure in Millions of U.S. Dollars, 1972-2000[191]

Year	Total Expenditure	Year	Total Expenditure
1972	328.1	1987	2,346.6
1973	496.1	1988	1,968.6
1974	847.8	1989	1,871.6
1975	1,146.4	1990	2,147.1
1976	1,370.2	1991	2,170.2
1977	1,670.5	1992	2,197.8
1978	1,796.5	1993	2,704.3
1979	1,889.2	1994	3,181.9
1980	2,435.9	1995	4,150.8
1981	2,929.0	1996	4,096.0
1982	2,698.4	1997	4,105.8
1983	1,337.2	1998	3,923.3
1984	1,671.4	1999	3,614.1
1985	2,545.8	2000	3,376.8
1986	2,467.5		

State revenue aside, Ecuador's macroeconomic performance also considerably improved with oil production. The gross domestic product of the country as measured in current United States dollars (not adjusted for inflation) increased at a spectacular average annual rate of 22.7% from 1972 to 1980 (see table 44). Total economic output increased from $4.3 billion in 1970 to over $10 billion in 1979. This growth rate not

---

[191] *Indices económicos del Ecuador. Country Statistics.*

experienced ever before in the nation's history was significantly felt across the country, which together with state investments, resulted in projects like rural electrification, universities, and local government funding, all of which received a portion of the newfound monies. Investment yielded an increase in the electrical power capacity, which increased from 304,000 kilowatts to 1,682,000 kilowatts during military rule.[192] Likewise, to signal another result of these circumstances, the illiteracy rate decreased from 31% to 13%. However, it was the military itself that received the largest share of oil revenues by far. From 1972 to 2000, 45% of this income went to the Armed Forces, who removed the funds from congressional oversight and from budgets approved by congress, and used them to create their own industrial enterprise (DINE), a petroleum transportation fleet (FLOPEC), and a commercial airline (TAME).[193]

Table 44: Ecuador GDP in current billions of U.S. dollars, 1971-2000[194]

Year	GDP	Year	GDP
1971	1.620	1986	11.310
1972	1.932	1987	9.099
1973	2.594	1988	9.098
1974	3.928	1989	9.528
1975	4.651	1990	10.356
1976	5.687	1991	11.348
1977	6.925	1992	11.997
1978	7,779	1993	15.063
1979	9.589	1994	18.582
1980	11.901	1995	20.206
1981	13.975	1996	21.278
1982	13.194	1997	23.647
1983	11,188	1998	23.266
1984	11.387	1999	16.682
1985	11.841	2000	15.942

The military government had elaborate plans to modernize Ecuador. Guillermo Rodriguez Lara believed that Ecuador required "decisive

[192] Dobronski, *El Ecuador: Los hechos más importantes de su historia*, 342.

[193] Gerlach, *Indians, Oil, and Politics*, 36.

[194] "Data: Ecuador," The World Bank. Accessed August 17, 2012. http://data.worldbank.org/country/ecuador.

intervention by the state in the economy to promote reforms necessary for national development. The strategy...meant transferring from foreign hands to the public sector the fundamental decisions affecting the economy and society."[195] Thus in 1972, the *Junta of Economic Planning and Coordination* presented a five-year plan for development in which the state would assume an active participation in the country's productive process.

Accordingly, under military rule the state's role in the economy reached its peak. During these governments, the state took control, either wholly or partially, of a wide array of economic activities, made possible due to the oil windfall that guaranteed the financial independence of the central government. This freedom enjoyed by the government, diminished power from the traditional Ecuadorian elite who previously controlled much of the nation's economical and political resources. Like this, the military expanded its ever-growing presence in the oil industry, and acquired interests in telephone service, electricity and gas utilities, airlines, fishing industry, leading sectors of agriculture (such as sugar, dairy, fertilizers, and seed production), tourism, textiles, munitions, hotels, travel agencies, banks, and steel. Moreover, the government used the considerable resources at their disposal to build roads at an unprecedented rate, provide credit for agricultural development, supply incentives for industry and manufacturing, and modernize the Armed Forces through the purchase of expensive military equipment.

Needless to say, those who governed Ecuador at the onset of petroleum wealth saw the commodity as a means to escape underdevelopment and poverty, and as a means to achieve a dynamic, developed, industrialized, and modern nation. The military governments strongly favored an import-substitution policy where high import taxes were expected to discourage the importation of cheap goods as well as develop local industry and create jobs. Additionally, high percentages of the state's budget were aimed at stimulating the local economy. Before 1972, the state's involvement in the economy was limited to the production of fertilizer and other small industries, and accounted for only 2% of the gross national product. By 1972, state involvement in the economy was at a level of 16%, and would reach 23%, the highest level

---

[195] Gerlach, *Indians, Oil, and Politics*, 38.

ever, in 1976,[196] with most of the government's industries being in the petroleum sector, as well as in transportation, communications, and utilities. Further still, the oil windfall was used to create a vast array of subsidies that were aimed at stimulating economic expansion and satisfying consumer demand. By 1978, nearly 50% of the state's budget was directed at food and energy subsidies, exemptions, and credits.[197]

The military government's attempts at modernization, at first glance, seemed to have worked well. Ecuador experienced growth in industrialization, increasing at an annual rate of 10.5%, by 1980 industry accounted for about 20% of the nation's gross domestic product. GDP itself nearly quintupled between 1972 and 1979 while factories bloomed around major cities. The state's subsidies provided cheap cooking fuel, electricity, and transportation, as well as gasoline that was sold to the public at less than one-half the cost of production. Investment in roads resulted in greater economic activity and movement of people. The number of automobiles increased from 82,000 vehicles in 1970 to 223,000 in 1977.[198] Prosperity was growing because of the windfall of oil and the titanic spending habits of the central government. So much was this the case, that the Ecuadorian Amazon transformed its garnered mythical characteristic into one of the eternal oil fields of the *oriente*. Talk among Ecuadorians alleged that reserves surpassed those of Venezuela and the Middle East, and that the wealth of black gold would only continue to bless Ecuador for a long time to come. Ecuadorians were happy, and the ever-increasing amounts of money assured stability during the 1970s, yet a continuous habit of underwriting by the government would eventually take its toll on the country.

Debt, Financial Problems and Instability

On October 6, 1973, a coalition of Arab states led by Egypt and Syria launched an attack on Israel. The attack coincided with Yom Kippur, the holiest day in Judaism, as well as with the Muslim holy month of Ramadan. The conflict, known as the Yom Kippur War, or Ramadan War, ended in an Israeli victory that was staunchly supported by the United

---

[196] Pineo, *Useful Strangers*, 2208. Industry reached a level of 12% of GNP in 1983 according to Allen Gerlach, *Indians, Oil, and Politics*, 37.

[197] Gerlach, *Indians, Oil, and Politics*, 37.

[198] Gerlach, *Indians, Oil, and Politics*, 38.

States. The outcome of this conflict would continue into the 21st century as one of the most complicated and dangerous divergences in the world. In the immediate aftermath, however, the consequences of the Israeli victory would prove disastrous for the world economy, and especially to those nations that were dependent on oil imports. Moral and political disagreements would influence the commodity market.

The Organization of Petroleum Exporting Countries (OPEC) was launched in 1960 with headquarters in Vienna, and with the purpose of expanding revenue in oil-producing nations. Ecuador joined the ranks of the organization in 1973 just before the oil embargo. The oil embargo was the retaliation action by Arab nations who were outraged at the support of Israel by the United States and other Western nations. Accordingly, member states would stop providing oil to those nations that had supported Israel. Supported by OPEC, the embargo would skyrocket oil prices, contribute to a worldwide recession, and change the panorama of international relations as oil-producing countries discovered that petroleum could be used as a political and economic weapon.

The oil embargo would last five months, from October 1973 until March 1974, yet the price hike initiated by it would continue into the 1980s. The multiplication of income generated by oil-producing nations, particularly by the larger Arab producers, resulted in ever-increasing monetary reserves. These reserves ended up in gargantuan public and private bank accounts within the leading financial institutions of the United States, Europe, and Japan. These funds became known as petrodollars, and the brokers that learned to operate them in New York, London, and Tokyo became known as yuppies.

Deposits in transnational banks increased 437% within five years from 1975 to 1980,[199] and with this massive increase in available funds came changes in legislation. To make money out of petrodollars, nations with the leading financial entities revised their trade laws. For instance: Germany eliminated limits in interest payments for non-residents and enabled them to invest in state bonds; France eliminated all obstacles for the repatriation of capital goods and eliminated a tax imposed on currency transactions; Great Britain removed exchange controls over financial transactions and allowed foreign companies to operate within

---

[199] Alfredo Vergara, *América Latina, entre sombras y luces* (Quito, Ecuador: Paradiso Editores, 2003), 12.

national borders; Japan approved the *Gensaki Statute*, which authorized foreigners to own and invest in capital goods within the country; and the United States passed a law of national treatment, which essentially meant that foreigners and locals were to be treated equally, and which meant that foreign banks could therefore freely and equally operate in the country.

As it happened, petrodollars changed international banking, and banks holding massive deposits saw this as an opportunity to maximize profits in a global market. During the 1970s, over 400 banks in developed nations granted loans to the developing world, out of which 10 would come to control over half the Latin American debt: Manufactures Hanover; Continental Illinois; First Chicago; Bank of America; Citigroup; Bankers Trust; Lloyds Bank, Chase Manhattan, Chemical, and Morgan Guaranty (now operating as JP Morgan Chase).[200] Therefore, credit became easy and governments welcomed the opportunity to cover commercial and budget deficits without having to raise taxes, issue currency, or adopt policies of austerity. Further, nations with increasing revenue—that is, oil exporting countries like Ecuador—were targeted by financial institutions because they were considered to have higher repayment capacities. Like this, oil countries in Latin America (Ecuador, Mexico, Venezuela) increased their debts by an average yearly rate of 25% during the 1970s, whereas the rest of the region increased debt at an average rate of 15%.[200]

Ecuador itself increased debt by an average yearly rate of 34.8% during the 1972 to 1979 military rule (see table 45). During the entire decade, the nation's foreign debt would multiply twenty times. Of all the development in Ecuador that would be emphasized by the military governments, the main expansion was that of debt. While Ecuador achieved a balanced budget in 1970, every year thereafter would be ones where expenditures exceeded income. Just a year later, in 1971, expenditure would surpass income by $15 million. By 1980, the budget had inflated to the point where the government spent $642 million more than what it took in.[201] Ecuador's own capital, even with a petroleum boom, was insufficient to sustain the aggressive import-substitution policies and modernization ambitions of the military governments. Hence, the state resorted to their

---

[200] Vergara, *América Latina, Entre Sombras Y Luces*, 14.

[201] Gerlach, *Indians, Oil, and Politics*, 40.

newfound wealth to secure foreign credit by offering oil reserves as collateral. Naturally, banks did not hesitate to seize the opportunity to profit from their newfound petrodollar deposits.

Table 45: Ecuador foreign debt, 1972-2001[202]

Year	Total Debt (millions of USD)	Year	Total Debt (millions of USD)
1972	260.8	1987	9,062.7
1973	343.9	1988	9,858.3
1974	380.4	1989	9,750.0
1975	410.0	1990	10,076.7
1976	512.7	1991	10,298.1
1977	693.1	1992	10,367.3
1978	1,675.8	1993	10,078.7
1979	2,974.6	1994	10,433.0
1980	3,554.1	1995	11,268.8
1981	4,651.7	1996	13,906.2
1982	5,869.8	1997	14,488.9
1983	6,632.8	1998	15,015.2
1984	7,380.7	1999	16,221.4
1985	7,596.0	2000	15,902.3
1986	8,110.7	2001	13,216.2

The country became bloated and inefficient. GDP growth was rising, but debt accumulation was rising even more. Ecuador's foreign debt to GDP ratio continually increased during the 1970s, rising from a rate of 13.5% of GDP in 1972 to a rate of 31.02% in 1979, and placing the country into a downward spiral that would afflict its finances for the rest of the century (see table 46). The size of government expanded from $133.7 million in salaries and wages in 1972, to a $209.5 million-100,000 employee apparatus in 1974, and into a bloated expense of over half a billion dollars in 1979, an average 18.9% yearly increase in 7 years (see table 50). Money was indeed injected into the economy, but government policies of trade restrictions and uncontrolled spending, would yield a result far different from what the Ecuadorian people expected at the beginning of the 1970s.

---

[202] *Indices económicos del Ecuador. Country Statistics.*

Table 46: Ecuador's foreign debt as percentage of GDP, 1972-2000[203]

Year	Total Debt (millions of USD)	Year	Total Debt (millions of USD)
1972	13.50%	1987	99.60%
1973	13.26%	1988	108.36%
1974	9.68%	1989	102.33%
1975	8.82%	1990	97.30%
1976	9.02%	1991	90.75%
1977	10.01%	1992	86.42%
1978	0.02%	1993	66.91%
1979	31.02%	1994	56.15%
1980	29.86%	1995	55.77%
1981	33.29%	1996	65.35%
1982	44.49%	1997	61.27%
1983	59.29%	1998	64.54%
1984	64.82%	1999	97.24%
1985	64.15%	2000	99.75%
1986	71.71%		

203 Calculated from data in: *Indices económicos del Ecuador. Country Statistics;* and "Data: Ecuador." The World Bank.

Table 47: Government expenditure of salaries and wages in millions of U.S. dollars, 1972-2001[204]

Year	Total Expenditure	Year	Total Expenditure
1972	133.7	1987	676.9
1973	143.6	1988	571.9
1974	209.5	1989	515.2
1975	302.2	1990	486.1
1976	362.3	1991	580.0
1977	384.7	1992	557.5
1978	430.1	1993	623.7
1979	501.5	1994	647.2
1980	760.3	1995	688.4
1981	927.2	1996	1,359.7
1982	861.6	1997	1,387.2
1983	437.3	1998	1,110.9
1984	524.7	1999	915.6
1985	621.9	2000	1,041.3
1986	717.3	2001	1,137.3

Through the first decade of oil, increased spending by way of debt accumulation assured the government could maintain stability and a hold on power. In the mid-1970s, a slumping economy was kept afloat through government expenditure financed by the oil industry. However, when the Texaco-Gulf consortium boycotted production in 1976, it became evident how fragile the country really was, and how dependent on oil it had become. The boycott was a terrible occurrence for Ecuadorian state finances. As it happened, the responsibilities of drilling and pumping petroleum rested, almost exclusively, in the hands of foreign companies, especially Texaco-Gulf. So when they decided to halt production in 1976 in retaliation to CEPEs exaggerated, restrictive regulations, Ecuadorian oil production was severely depleted and consequently emptied government coffers.

The problem with the oil companies had begun almost immediately after production began in 1972. Only two years into the oil bonanza, CEPE increasingly tried to secure a larger and larger share of the profits from the multinationals to the point where by 1974 these companies had become increasingly irritated. Not even the firing of CEPEs manager, Gustavo Jarrin, in 1974 eased the situation. And so by 1975, because of problems

[204] *Indices económicos del Ecuador. Country Statistics.*

with Texaco-Gulf, exports fell by 50% and depleted government revenue by the same rate. A massive general strike soon followed while the elite began transferring their money oversees. As the unrest intensified in the following months, the military became divided and General Raul González Alvear led a coup attempt in August 1975 known as the "funeral parlor revolt" because it was planned at such a place. One hundred civilian casualties resulted from the operation as innocent bystanders were shot by automatic weapons near the presidential palace.

The coup failed, but it was becoming clear that the administration of Rodriguez Lara had lost support, and Rear Admiral Alfredo Poveda Burbano made another attempt at replacing him on January 1976. This second effort was successful and General Guillermo Rodriguez Lara was forced to resign and replaced by another military administration, which was accepted by the public due to their vow of returning the nation to democracy. In this way, because of the financial burden brought forth by the problems arising with oil production, Ecuador's head of state and his government had fallen. Quickly, the plan that was supposed to modernize Ecuador was abandoned. First, the new administration turned its attention into replacing people in main government posts. Then, projects like that of agrarian reform, which proved to be an utter and complete failure, were eliminated.

Even with a change in leadership, the economy and oil production continued to suffer. Oil prices were beginning to stagnate and discoveries became less frequent, and by 1979 the amount of production that was exported decreased by about 50%. With a slumping economy towards the end of the decade, the second military government to rule Ecuador in the 1970s prepared to relinquish power back to a democratically elected president. In 1979 a new constitution was written and a new president was elected, but the military would spend their last months in power by going on a wasteful spending spree with borrowed money. By 1980, Ecuador's debt was twice as much as it was in 1978, and twenty times as much as it was in 1970. Debt servicing as a percentage of exports rose from 5% in 1977 to 23% in 1981.[205] Like this, with the oil boom coming to an end, and with debts piling up, the military would return to their barracks.

---

[205] Pineo, *Useful Strangers*, 2244.

Crises Develop

After seven years of military rule, Ecuador went back to civilian governance. A new constitution was in place, and elections were carried out on July 16, 1978. However not all went smoothly, and before the military finally transferred power, Ecuador would go through two significant events. On November 29, defeated presidential candidate, Abdón Calderón Muñoz was assassinated after making harsh accusations against the government. This incident, perhaps the greatest blow to freedom in Ecuador during the military regime, would somehow be forgotten later on, on July 27th, when Quito would be officially proclaimed (the proclamation had been announced on September 8, 1978) UNESCO's first World Heritage Center along with the Galapagos Islands. This latter occurrence represented one of the country's proudest moments and almost completely overshadowed the devastating episode of a few months earlier. The following August, the Supreme government council of the military government would finally withdraw from power.

The winning presidential candidate of the 1979 elections, Jaime Roldós Aguilera (1979-1981), took office on August 10, 1979. Together with the presidential band, he would inherit the government of a nation entering a deep and troublesome financial crisis that would last nearly a decade, and whose debt accumulation would haunt the country into the 21st century. Ecuador's foreign financial obligations stood at an all-time high of nearly $3 billion, equivalent to 31.02% of GDP. Nevertheless, oil prices continued their upward hike, and because of it, the government was able to control its budget even when 9.16% of government expenditure had to be destined to meet debt interest payments (see table 48).

Table 48: Government disbursements of interest payments, 1972-2000[206]

Year	Absolute Amount	% of total government expenditure	Year	Absolute Amount	% of total government expenditure
1972	22.4	6.81%	1987	242.3	10.33%
1973	27.5	5.55%	1988	254.7	12.94%
1974	32.1	3.78%	1989	322.1	17.21%
1975	31.8	2.77%	1990	448.4	20.88%
1976	58.0	4.24%	1991	330.2	15.21%
1977	75.6	4.52%	1992	333.4	15.17%
1978	102.4	5.70%	1993	266.6	9.86%
1979	173.1	9.16%	1994	427.4	13.43%
1980	137.6	5.65%	1995	852.9	20.55%
1981	245.8	8.39%	1996	616.5	15.05%
1982	352.1	13.05%	1997	939.8	22.89%
1983	220.1	16.46%	1998	705.3	17.98%
1984	235.0	14.06%	1999	681.4	18.85%
1985	415.4	16.32%	2000	789.0	23.37%
1986	340.8	13.81%			

As the 1980s began, the Ecuadorian economy, the state, and the general population alike continued to rely on petroleum exports and on the increasing availability of credit offered by lending institutions. In point of fact, growth depended on oil and credit, and as such, interest payments on debt would continue to rise throughout the rest of the 20th century. With this dependency, the country was sailing in dangerous waters, and naturally, the country could only stay afloat as long as petroleum exports remained high and credit kept coming. It was not unfortunate then that the escalation of Ecuador's conflict with its southern neighbor came at a time when Ecuador had been spending a great percentage of its oil wealth on military equipment, and when the high price of oil assured that the government still had the necessary funding from exports to withstand a belligerence.

During the dictatorship of Peruvian General Velasco Alvarado (1968-1975), Peru took on a remarkable spending binge in military equipment. Purchasing arms primarily from the Soviet Union, Peru increased its

[206] *Indices económicos del Ecuador. Country Statistics.*

military budget 350% between 1966 and 1976.[207] Between 1971 and 1975, years when the Ecuadorian military dictatorship drastically increased military spending, Peru spent almost four times as much. After 1975, Peru further increased its military buildup hinting at a probable military conflict. While analysts could have presumed Peru's military spending was aimed at a war with Chile, given the one-hundred-year anniversary of the war of the Pacific that had been fought with that nation, Peru's attention was unequivocally directed towards Ecuador.

On January 28, 1981, Peruvian helicopters attacked Ecuadorian outposts in Paquisha with the purpose of capturing it and two others. Peru wanted to legitimize the 1941 Rio Protocol while Ecuador would continually challenge it. Although the Peruvian army once again outnumbered the Ecuadorian, Ecuador was in a much better position to defend itself against its aggressor than it had been in 1941. Not only was the military better equipped, but also the country's diplomacy was in top form. In point of fact, it was Ecuador's diplomatic body that proved decisive in attaining a cease-fire agreement and support from friendly nations, even when Peru refused mediation. Thus, even when Peru broke the cease-fire agreement on February 19[208] and advanced its attack towards the Range of *El Condor*, Ecuador was able to broker a withdrawal from confrontation and put an end to the 1981 Paquisha incident.

A stronger government, result of a stronger economy, was able to set forth a stronger military and a sturdier diplomacy, and avert an undesirable outcome of the likes Ecuador endured in 1941. After the Paquisha incident, nationalist sentiments ran high, even more with President Roldós addressing the incident with Peru in his most famous speech at the Atahualpa Olympic stadium in Quito. Nevertheless, debts were still increasing while the price of petroleum did not. In 1981, oil prices began to decline and their descent was as dramatic as their ascent had been. After reaching its apex in 1980, prices would continually decrease until 1989. As a matter of fact, the price of WTI crude decreased by 57.8% from 1980 to 1988. With the nation's financial stability succumbing, Vice President Osvaldo Hurtado assumed the presidency on May 24, 1981 after the aircraft carrying President Roldós, his wife, and

---

[207] Academia Nacional De Historia Militar, comp., *Historia militar del Ecuador*, 521.

[208] Peru claimed Ecuador broke the Cease-fire agreement.

most of the cabinet, crashed after leaving Quito the same day of his memorable speech.

Hurtado received a country on a path to financial disarray. The nation experienced, from 1975 and into the 1990s, a steady decline in potential GDP growth rate (6.4% annually from 1975-1980, to 1.8% in the early 1990s)[209]. Ecuador's debt, was taking an ever-growing share of the state's budget, standing at almost $5 billion and increasing. Like other Latin American nations, Ecuador could not handle the vast amount of borrowed money, especially with high interest rates and short-term conditions, which were made even worse after the collapse of the overextended Mexican economy in 1982. Inflation began to severely increase. In 1983 this rate increased from 28.3% to 63.4%,[210] a trend that would continue for the rest of the century, developing into one of Ecuador's foremost problems. In point of fact, in the half a decade following 1983, the exchange rate of the Ecuadorian Sucre would decrease at an annual rate of 29.63% with respect to the U.S. dollar. Furthermore, and as it seems to often to occur in history, bad times attract further disasters. On top of the financial crisis plaguing Ecuador, a devastating 10-month winter in 1983 due to the *El Niño* phenomenon ruined crops across the country, destroyed roads, and further delivered a blow into an already wounded nation. Hurtado could not do much to correct the debilitating situation of the Ecuadorian economy, and would transfer a country with the same problems to Leon Febres Cordero (1984-1988) in 1984.

---

[209] Erik Offerdal, Mariano Cortés, Mayra Zermeño, Alvin Hilaire, Gabriela Inchauste, Fernando Delgado, Antonio Pancorbo, and Werner Keller. *Ecuador: Selected Issues and Statistical Annex.*

[210] Dobronski, *El Ecuador: Los hechos más importantes de su historia*, 345.

Table 49: Exchange rate of Ecuadorian sucre vs. U.S. dollar, 1972-2000[211]

Year	Exchange Rate	Year	Exchange Rate
1972	24.75	1987	95.00
1973	24.80	1988	194.45
1974	24.80	1989	390.00
1975	24.80	1990	390.00
1976	24.80	1991	390.00
1977	24.80	1992	390.00
1978	24.80	1993	394.41
1979	24.80	1994	2,192.72
1980	24.80	1995	2,552.09
1981	24.80	1996	3,176.55
1982	30.00	1997	3,983.07
1983	44.20	1998	5,402.94
1984	62.30	1999	11,547.82
1985	70.38	2000	25,000.00*
1986	95.00		

*** In 2000, convertibility was set at 25,000 sucres per 1 U.S. dollar as the process of dollarization of the Ecuadorian economy was installed.**

By the mid 1980s the prosperity of the oil-driven 1970s had vanished. The money that was borrowed was all gone as well—sometimes spent wisely, but more often than not the money was squandered or fallen under the gloomy hands of corruption—but gone nonetheless. As most Latin American nations, Ecuador found itself unable to service its considerable debt obligations. Consequently, the Febres Cordero government decided it had no choice but to borrow more money in order to pay off the interest. Unlike the previous decade, however, banks were not eager to grant credits to a crises ridden region that Ecuador was part of. Thus, before Ecuador and other Latin American nations could get new loans, they had to carry out economic reforms approved by the international banking community and handled by the International Monetary Fund.

Accordingly, the Febres Cordero government would try to become one of compliance with IMF reforms. Just like the Kemmerer mission's recommendations in the 1920s, the IMF's recommendations followed the economic orthodoxies of the time, namely fiscal austerity and free market

---

211 *Indices económicos del Ecuador. Country Statistics.*

policies. In Latin America, these measures principally meant privatizing state-owned companies, cutting government spending, eliminating price controls and subsidies, lowering and/or eliminating tariffs, opening up to foreign investors, and raising taxes to pay the interest due on foreign loans. These policies were later coined under the tendencies of *neoliberalism* practiced under the "Washington Consensus," which were championed by the leading financial institutions, and most of all by the political and financial authorities of the United States.

To these reforms, Ecuador never completely complied. Although a process of privatization was successfully put in place, transferring state owned firms into healthy private ones, other aspects of the IMF recommendations went ignored. Principally among the recommendations to which Ecuador turned a blind eye were those of fiscal austerity. Although from 1981 forwards, Ecuadorian governments actually did enact austerity programs, which cut expenditure in subsidies, services and even on health and education, the fact is that Ecuador failed to adequately reduce spending and restrict state involvement in the economy. As a result, the country experienced stagnation under the heavy burdens of debt, inflation, and unstable oil prices.

The IMF, in a 2000 report on Ecuador made emphasis on the "longstanding structural weaknesses" inhibiting Ecuador's development. Most of these included unfulfilled reforms from the 1980s such as "connected lending and fraudulent practices" in the banking sector. High hiring and firing costs in the labor market; weak tax legislation and administration; a restricted trade system with high tariffs, and regulated prices on several commodities and utilities. Significantly, the IMF mentioned the problems facing development of the oil sector in Ecuador because of the restrictions on foreign investment in the oil industry, particularly regarding the state monopoly in transshipment of petroleum products through the oil pipeline[212].

Febres Cordero took office in 1984 and immediately obtained $105 million from the IMF in 1985 after adopting a restrictive monetary policy. The following year he failed to receive the requested $91 million, and only received 20% of that amount because the government's fiscal policies fell short of IMF expectations, even when gasoline prices increased 80% as a

---

212 Offerdal, Cortés, Zermeño, Hilaire, Inchauste, Delgado, Pancorbo, Keller. *Ecuador: Selected Issues and Statistical Annex.*

result of an elimination of subsidies and even when the minimum wage was set lower than what had been established by congress.[213] The Febres Cordero government, it could be argued, tried to please the IMF but the Fund's strict impositions and other external circumstances could not avert a crisis. During Febres Cordero's term, petroleum prices dropped at an average of 15.25% per year. Moreover, an earthquake on March 4, 1987, caused the nation's only pipeline to burst and halt oil production. Consequently, petroleum exports froze for over five months, which meant that the nation stopped receiving revenue from its main source of income. Government proceeds dropped 60% in 1987.

The majority of the crisis of the 1980s took place during the Febres Cordero government. Although the IMF was constantly unsatisfied with the government's enacting of recommended policies, the country still borrowed money given that lenders and the Ecuadorian government alike wrongly believed that the country could repay the advances with the ever-expanding oil revenue. Like this, Ecuador would increase its debt burden and with it its interest obligations. The budget would suffer as a result, and so the country would have its last budget surplus in 1985. From then on, the country would run a deficit every year. When Febres Cordero left office, the nation was deeply in debt with the figure rising to 108.36% of GDP. The nation's monetary reserve was boasting a red figure of $330 million, the budget deficit ran at 490 billion sucres, and the exchange operations by the Central Bank of Ecuador registered a loss of 877 billion sucres.[214]

In 1988, Rodrigo Borja Cevallos (1988-1992) would have an opportunity to remedy Ecuador's situation. Burdened with debt, and with the straightjacket that this implied, Borja had no choice but to continue under the recommendations of the IMF. A staunch critic of his predecessor, Borja ran a campaign in which he pledged to pay the social debt by improving health and other social assistance programs. However, he was unable to fulfill his pledge and, albeit more gradually, continued the policies of his predecessor. Currency continued to be devaluated and loans continued to accrue in order to pay off interest payments. Petroleum prices remained low, which assured that inflation continued its upward direction while strikes across the country remained common.

---

[213] Gerlach, *Indians, Oil, and Politics*, 44.

[214] Dobronski, *El Ecuador: Los hechos más importantes de su historia*, 348.

Every January, rises in the cost of basic necessities known as the *paquetazos*, became common in order to comply with the IMF demands of austerity. Together with decreasing minimum wages (see table 50), the rising cost of living had a terrible impact on the country's disadvantaged.

Table 50: Minimum wage by year, 1972-2001[215]

Year	Amount in Sucres	Amount in U.S. Dollars	Year	Amount in Sucres	Amount in U.S. Dollars
1972	750	29	1987	12,000	82
1973	750	30	1988	14,500	54
1974	1,000	40	1989	22,000	41
1975	1,000	40	1990	32,000	39
1976	1,500	56	1991	40,000	36
1977	1,500	55	1992	40,000	30
1978	1,500	56	1993	60,000	32
1979	2,000	72	1994	66,000	32
1980	4,000	144	1995	75,000	32
1981	4,000	128	1996	95,000	30
1982	4,000	115	1997	95,000	24
1983	4,600	69	1998	100,000	18
1984	6,600	67	1999	100,000	8
1985	6,600	54	2000	100,000	4
1986	10,000	76	2001	--	85.7

During the 1980s, the oil opulence of the 1970s lay forgotten. The slogan *we were better off when we were worse off* became popular while the industrial sector grew a mere 0.2% per year.[216] Foreign capital also struggled to contribute to Ecuador's economy as capitalists deemed the market too small for significant profits. Furthermore, investors considered Ecuador's industry overprotected and noncompetitive compared to that of other countries in the region.[216] By 1992, Borja would finish his term in office with a literacy program among his greatest accomplishments. However, the financial situation had not changed much.

---

[215] *Indices Económicos del Ecuador*. Country Statistics.

[216] Gerlach, *Indians, Oil, and Politics*, 41.

Stabilization, Growth, and Recommenced Havoc

With oil prices constant, debts, and interest payments piling up, Sixto Durán Ballén (1992-1996) assumed the presidency on August 10, 1992. With the straightjacket of debt still in place, the government had to find another way to make Ecuador's economy prosper. This came in the form of following the other IMF recommendations, that is, not just cutting back spending, but privatizing unproductive government enterprises, opening markets, and encouraging investment. From 1988 to 1995, Ecuador privatized eleven public companies worth about $169 million.[217] But more importantly, Ecuador opened up to the world, encouraging investment and liberalizing restrictions through its accession to the World Trade Organization. Ecuador signed its adhesion to the WTO on September 27, 1995, after a series of intense and difficult negotiations led by Durán Ballén's vice-minister of foreign relations, Patricio Izurieta Mora-Bowen.

Potential for trade increased during the Durán-Ballén government. The production possibilities frontier curve for Ecuador expanded with increased commerce, as better exchange practices elevated the production of capital and consumer goods. During the Durán Ballén government, non-petroleum products exports increased by an average of 14.3% per year, while they had increased at a level of 9.17% per year during the previous administration (see table 51). Furthermore, the increasing opening to the world market also increased exportations to non-traditional markets in Europe and Asia (see table 52). And with the price of oil in stagnation, Ecuador was able to significantly increase GDP for the first time in a decade, 77.4% from 1992 to 1996, compared with the contraction of 9.1% experienced during the decade from 1982 to 1992 that also resulted in a 27% increase in poverty levels.[218]

The country's healthy situation was further boosted after another confrontation with Peru resulted in an unequivocal victory for Ecuadorians, eliminating the bitter aftertastes of previous conflicts and discharging intense feelings of national pride. Peru invaded Ecuador in order to reaffirm their view of the 1941 Rio Protocol, yet they were unable to capture their objectives in the disputed territories. *Ni un paso atrás* (not one step back) became the national slogan during the war as the

---

[217] Pineo, *Useful Strangers*, 2468.

[218] Gerlach, *Indians, Oil, and Politics*, 46.

Ecuadorian forces defended the front, the *Alto Cenepa* and *Tiwintza*, despite being outnumbered by the Peruvian military. A modernized military and the creation of a special operations unit proved pivotal in Ecuador's defense strategies.

Table 51: Total Non-Petroleum Exports in U.S. dollars, 1972-2001[219]

Year	Total Exports x 1000	Year	Total Exports x 1000
1972	266,392	1987	1,203,706
1973	249,302	1988	1,216,721
1974	426,828	1989	1,206,443
1975	309,937	1990	1,305,749
1976	386,404	1991	1,699,293
1977	718,167	1992	1,756,200
1978	779,823	1993	1,808,962
1979	991,073	1994	2,537,855
1980	919,656	1995	2,850,769
1981	815,773	1996	3,123,973
1982	710,334	1997	3,707,097
1983	573,070	1998	3,280,104
1984	785,782	1999	2,971,402
1985	978,157	2000	2,484,203
1986	1,203,340	2001	2,778,442

219 *Indices económicos del Ecuador.* Country Statistics.

Table 52: Exports by destination in millions of U.S. dollars, 1972-2001[220]

Year	Total Exports	Exports to U.S.A.	Exports to E.U.	Exports to Asia
1972	326.3	112.7	63.1	53.1
1973	532.0	181.4	68.9	23.0
1974	1,123.5	459.8	125.7	23.0
1975	897.1	419.9	86.2	20.4
1976	1,127.3	391.6	125.5	30.9
1977	1,436.3	626.2	207.0	34.8
1978	1,493.8	668.6	222.2	47.9
1979	2,172.7	759.5	207.5	48.7
1980	2,506.2	748.6	207.2	314.9
1981	2,541.4	963.8	119.3	839.3
1982	2,237.4	945.7	65.2	459.1
1983	2,225.6	1,163.4	60.8	374.8
1984	2,620.4	1,725.7	89.7	470.4
1985	2,904.7	1,659.0	131.8	737.7
1986	2,185.8	1,332.6	173.9	369.8
1987	1,929.2	1,056.4	148.0	246.7
1988	2,193.5	1,006.2	202.6	338.4
1989	2,353.9	1,367.6	208.4	156.0
1990	2,724.1	1,585.0	272.9	148.2
1991	2,851.0	1,312.8	481.6	414.4
1992	3,101.5	1,326.0	488.2	491.6
1993	3,065.6	1,305.1	502.4	397.6
1994	3,842.7	1,594.2	753.0	403.9
1995	4,380.7	1,759.2	844.2	483.6
1996	4,872.6	1,859.0	943.2	603.3
1997	5,264.4	2,032.1	1,017.1	574.7
1998	4,203.0	1,637.2	872.4	344.6
1999	4,451.1	1,708.1	817.9	492.1
2000	4,926.6	1,874.7	610.9	579.1
2001	4,678.4	1,789.7	666.3	445.8

Sixto Durán Ballén placed the presidential band on his successor, Abdalá Bucaram Ortiz on August 10, 1996. Known as *El Loco* (the crazy one), Abdalá became known more for his antics than for his politics. Carrying a campaign aimed at the underclass, he would arrive at rallies by helicopter, singing and accompanied by go-go dancers. He would eat typical Ecuadorian dishes and hug his fellow citizens with apparent

[220] *Indices económicos del Ecuador. Country Statistics.*

passion. At his rallies, as the moment intensified, he would strip to the waist and deliver over the top speeches that would induce tears among his supporters. Outrageous claims, like one where he attested having superior sperm than that of his effeminate adversaries, were also common within his speeches. Regarding his political policy, he promised increased government subsidies and social programs aimed at helping the nation's underprivileged.

Bucaram lasted six months in office. After adopting an austerity program four months into his presidency, his popularity began to decline as the price of basic goods and services began to radically increase. Public transportation costs increased 60%, gasoline 245%, electricity 300%, and telephone service 1000%.[221] The government also opted to raise taxes and continue the privatization of public companies, which went against the desires of his supporters. These blows took a toll on the nation's patience, and together with blatant corruption, to which U.S. ambassador Leslie Alexander asserted at the time that "Ecuador is gaining a reputation for pervasive corruption,"[222] Bucaram's approval rating nosedived to 5% in early 1997.

As a result, massive demonstrations against Bucaram and his government became almost daily events. On February 5, 1997, a mammoth nationwide general strike of over two million demonstrators took to the streets to demand the president's resignation. Roads were blocked and communication across the country thwarted. Schools and universities closed and Ecuador's economic activity halted. The country was up in arms, and even former presidents called for Bucaram's resignation. Perhaps the final blow came when the military, which had been used at the Guayaquil customs house and thus had become part of the government's corruption system, pronounced their disapproval of the president. The military's reputation was being damaged by association, and the officers did not like that.

Bucaram tried to lower the price hikes of basic goods and services but it was, as they say, a drowning man's last kick. Opposition forces in congress moved for impeachment, and on February 6, 1997, Bucaram was ousted on the grounds of "mental incapacity." This decision was unconstitutional because a supreme court judge had to order a psychiatric

---

[221] Pineo, *Useful Strangers*, 2468.

[222] Pineo, *Useful Strangers*, 2495.

examination before any elected official could be removed, and this process was never completed. Congress opted to qualify him as unfit to rule because the alternative, an investigation of the corruption allegations, would have taken too long and would have also implicated several congressmen.

Bucaram was out, and with him the political stability that began in 1972. For twenty-four years the country had experienced relative political stability, the military governed for seven years and then calmly transferred power to civilian rule in 1979, and after that, five presidents would come and go with no revolt as a cause for dismissal. But after Bucaram was overthrown, six presidents would assume office within ten years and none of them would serve a complete term. Vice-president Rosalía Arteaga would rule for five days following Bucaram, and interim president Fabian Alarcón (1997-1998) for two years after that. Following Alarcón, elections were held and Quito mayor Jamil Mahuad would assume office on August 10, 1998, after winning the presidential elections that year.

Mahuad will probably go down in history as the Ecuadorian president with the worst luck of the 20th century. When he assumed office in 1998, the price of oil hit an all time low, averaging a period price of $14.43 and hitting bottom at just over $6 a barrel.[223] Furthermore, he encountered a banking crisis in full swing due to the accelerated increment of bad loans that in turn resulted in the accelerated withdrawal of deposits in sucres with the objective of turning them into U.S. dollars. The origins of the banking fallout in Ecuador had its roots on widespread management incompetence allowed by the government because of its tendency to bail out banks instead of enforcing prudent practice standards. Ineffective supervision, lax legislation, and lack of enforcement, combined with a weak economy, assured that a systematic liquidity problem destroy the banking industry in Ecuador.

Needless to say, one of the nation's most important banks had gone bankrupt two months before he assumed the presidency, and another, the *Banco de Préstamos*, went bankrupt just two weeks into Mahuad's term on August 24, 1998. Further still, the 1998 *El Niño* was the worst in recent history and completely destroyed crops across the country, as well as roads and infrastructure. Moreover, the Russian crisis in the fall of 1998, and ensuing reassessment of emerging market risk by financial markets

---

[223] "West Texas Intermediate Oil Price (US$/Barrel)," Global Financial Data.

assured a further setback to Ecuador through the reduction in lines of credit. All the problems that could have delivered a blow to Ecuador hit the nation hard at its foundations. An outright financial crisis, political instability, natural disasters, and the debacle of the price of oil—Ecuador's main source of revenue by far—assured Ecuador would live through dreadful times.

During Mahuad's presidency, the number of bankrupt banks fell like dominos, one third of them were either taken by the government or closed altogether. One after another the government had to take charge of the insolvent institutions with money it simply did not have. No monetary reserve and no income from oil made it impossible for the government to adequately handle such a colossal financial crisis. In 1998, the economy shrunk by 1.6% vis-à-vis 1997. The following year GDP would experience an even greater contraction of 28.30%. By 2000, the economy had contracted by 32.58% in relation to 1997. Per capita GDP reached 1980 levels (see table 53) and unemployment rose from 9.2% in 1997 to 14% in 1999 (see table 54). Poverty as measured by an income of $2 per day reached an all-time high in 1999 with 39.24% of the population living in scarceness (see table 55).

Table 53: GDP per capita in current U.S. dollars, 1972-2001[224]

Year	GDP per capita	Year	GDP per capita
1972	305	1987	952
1973	398	1988	929
1974	585	1989	950
1975	673	1990	1,009
1976	800	1991	1,081
1977	947	1992	1,119
1978	1,034	1993	1,375
1979	1,239	1994	1,663
1980	1,495	1995	1,775
1981	1,709	1996	1,837
1982	1,570	1997	2,008
1983	1,296	1998	1,945
1984	1,285	1999	1,373
1985	1,303	2000	1,291
1986	1,106	2001	1,693

224 "World DataBank," The World Bank Databank. Accessed August 14, 2012. http://databank.worldbank.org/data/home.aspx.

Table 54: Percentage of total labor force unemployed, 1987-2001[225]

Year	Unemployment	Year	Unemployment
1987	7.2%	1994	7.1%
1988	7%	1995	6.9%
1989	7.9%	1996	10.4%
1990	6.1%	1997	9.2%
1991	5.8%	1999	14%
1992	8.9%	2000	9%
1993	8.3%	2001	10.7%

Table 55: Poverty headcount ratio at $2 a day for selected years, 1987-2000[226]

Year	Poverty Headcount Ratio	Year	Poverty Headcount Ratio
1987	23.03%	1998	27.17%
1994	26.33%	1999	39.24%
1995	20.39%	2000	37.71%

The Mahuad presidency's problems were many, and although most of them were not of the president's making, he was nevertheless blamed for them. The country was in shambles, and Mahuad's decision to adhere to the IMF recommendations and cut subsidies did not help his declining popularity, which by January 2000 would be down to a mere 7% approval. His decision to freeze bank accounts in 1999 in order to prevent a run on deposits outraged citizens. The astronomical inflation rates (the sucre dropped 362.7% in value from 1998 to 2000) meant that the value of deposits was largely reduced by the time accounts were finally able to be accessed. Mahuad also used $6 billion, about a quarter of GDP, in bailing out damaged banks. Yet most banks still went under and their wealthy owners fled the country. Together with the fact that the Mahuad campaign received a $3.1 million donation from the head of *Banco del Progreso*, one of Ecuador's leading banks, the measures taken to save the country from complete ruin were taken by most Ecuadorians as measures to save rich bankers at the expense of the rest.

The crisis affecting Ecuador at the end of the 20th century even overshadowed the 1998 peace treaty between Ecuador and Peru, a truly

225 "World DataBank," The World Bank Databank.

226 "World DataBank," The World Bank Databank.

remarkable act of statesmanship that put an end to 168 years of conflict with the southern neighbor. Ecuador finally became a nation in peace. Yet despite Mahuad's act of heroism, Ecuadorians grew ever more desperate because of the financial crisis, and by January 2000 his approval rating lay obliterated. One of his final acts while in office was the dollarization of the Ecuadorian economy, which was conceived in order to control the rampaging inflation. On January 21, junior military officers joined a sea of hostile Ecuadorian Indians to overthrow the president. The coup d'état was the first time in Ecuadorian history where the indigenous population had such a strong influence on the events. Mahuad was deposed and replaced by a military triumvirate that included future president Colonel Lucio Gutierrez. And like that, the dire financial circumstances in Ecuador would bring down another Ecuadorian president and destabilize the country at the eve of the 21st century. Jamil Mahuad would leave Ecuador to become a fellow at Harvard University in Cambridge, Massachusetts.

The last quarter century in Ecuador, just as the previous three, was a time in which the health of the economy was significantly tied to the performance of a single commodity. When the commodity did not perform, neither did the country. In fact, Ecuador never grew its economy in the 20th century without the increase of the three pillar commodity industries. More often than not, the behavior of the commodities Ecuador's economy has been dependent on determined the outcome of the major sociopolitical events in its history. Good times generated stability, while economic hardship generated political turmoil and upheavals. From the start of massive oil production in 1972 to the fall of Jamil Mahuad in 2000, Ecuador's destiny became unquestionably coupled with the price of petroleum. Oil production determined the capacity of obtaining foreign credit and of financing state budgets. Consequently, the performance of the black gold commodity determined the all-around health of the nation, with the clearest example being that of the 1998 banking crisis during the presidency of Jamil Mahuad.

Picture 20: Sixto delivering a speech addressing the 1995 conflict with Peru.

Picture 21: President Sixto Durán Ballén with Vice-minister Patricio Izurieta Mora-Bowen

Picture 22: Ecuadorian base at Tiwintza

Picture 23: Monument to the heroes of the 1995 victory against Peru.

Epilogue

Throughout Ecuadorian history, financial circumstances have had profound implications on major sociopolitical events. It was because of the cacao-fueled economy that the liberal era spearheaded by Eloy Alfaro was able to instill progressive ideals and reforms. It was through increased income from the cacao trade that the Ecuadorian railroad was built. Similarly, when the economy suffered, so did the political and social climate of the country. No other example is more obvious than the Julian Revolution in 1925, which happened as a consequence of a financial catastrophe. The same could be said about the negative outcome of the war fought in 1941, right after the gloomiest financial decade in Ecuadorian history. Financial circumstances also played a part in the sociopolitical and institutional stability enjoyed during the banana boom. Again, it was the wealth produced by the petroleum industry years later that catapulted Ecuador's biggest GDP growth of the century during the 1970s and the stability of governments thereafter.

These less than intricate correlations thus raise the question of what would the history of the country have looked like if the financial ups and downs had occurred at different times. For instance, after World War I, Ecuador began suffering from a decline in trade, which severely hampered the economy. In point of fact, customs revenue being the most important source of income for the government of the time was saved only because the United States took over the Ecuadorian export market. What would have become of the country had this not happened? Would the Julian Revolution that came a decade later have occurred in 1915? The same could be argued for future revolts during the 20th century. Would the *Gloriosa* Revolution in 1944 have taken place if Ecuador had not lost over half its territory to Peru? Probably not, but the defeat in 1941 against Peru was the direct consequence of an under-prepared and completely under-funded military. This was a result of deep financial troubles. The atrocious decade of the 1930s assured Ecuador was unable to properly equip its soldiers. Therefore, if the 1930s could have somehow resembled the prosperity of the 1970s, and the 1941 conflict that of the *Paquisha* war of 1981 or the *Alto* Cenepa fight of 1995, the *Gloriosa* may have never happened.

The same relationship exists with the degree of success of serving presidents. Why is it that the least successful presidents in all of 20th-century Ecuador occupied office in the troubled post-cacao decade of the 1930s? During this time fifteen heads of government took office. The periods after the banana bonanza and the petroleum boom also featured fragile heads of state. In point of fact, after the end of the banana boom, heads of state would begin to struggle until the prospect of a petroleum industry came knocking at the door. Black gold, as petroleum is fittingly referred to, ushered in a series of six presidents, none of which was overthrown, a unique feat in Ecuadorian history. Conversely, towards the end of the century, a series of unsuccessful presidents stepped in and out of the Carondelet palace due to a debilitating economy. An obvious example is that of Mahuad, who with the lowest oil rate of any president faced a horrifying economic situation in 1998.

It should also be noted, however, that historical events are never the product of just a single variable. Obvious as it seems that financial circumstances did in fact have significant implications on major events, other factors also played a role. We should not ignore the ideals surrounding the liberals during the start of the century. It may very well be that these ideals without financial backing would have had a different impact, but their existence should be acknowledged. And the same is true for future events and the leaders surrounding them. Although economic circumstances seem to have had a profound impact on the success of presidents, it is also obvious that different men have different talents. Alfaro's mystique, Velasco's discourse, Galo Plaza's statesmanship, Arroyo del Río's inattention, Durán Ballén's progressiveness, Bucaram's lunacy, all would have surely had different outcomes with matching conditions. Yet, these features by themselves do not account for the major political events here studied.

During the 1980s and 1990s, for instance, the declining oil prices and fickle economy were not the only factors determining major political events in Ecuador. The world was changing at a rapid pace, globalization was having its effect on all the economies of the world. Technology and economic integration became essential ingredients of a healthy economy. Insistence on import-substitution policies proved disastrous and Ecuador, like other countries, was forced to open its doors to the world in order to progress. Barriers separating national markets tumbled just as the Berlin Wall did in 1989. The information superhighway increased competitiveness as well as people's expectations for better standards of living, as they could now compare products and services from societies around the world. Henceforth, businesses and countries that remained insulated by government protectionism were bound to suffer devastating consequences.

As Ecuador entered the 21st century, the patterns that had defined it in the 20th continued. Unstable governments coincided with unstable finances, and the country remained dependent on a single commodity for financial health. Never have the effects of high oil prices been so evident than with the government of Rafael Correa. Correa assumed office on January 15, 2007, and became the first president since Sixto Durán Ballén to serve out a complete term in office. Not only did he complete his term, but he won three consecutive elections thereafter, one for the approval of a new government sponsored constitution, and the other two that reelected him as president.

His approval ratings have also constantly been among the best in Latin America, and his influence in Ecuadorian culture, and regional politics have been enviable from the viewpoint of an Ecuadorian leader. It should be no surprise, then, that his financial circumstances have been among the best in Ecuadorian history. Never has the price of Ecuadorian crude been higher than during the Correa government. By some estimates, income from oil during Correa is greater than that of all his predecessors combined.[227] As such, he has been able to finance several social programs and reforms backed up by a multi-million-dollar propaganda campaign that also distracts citizens from the all too recognizable practices of Ecuadorian presidents. Correa's financial condition has also allowed him to produce a hugely inflated bureaucratic contraption, prosecute unfavorable sectors of the press, and favor the interests of his political agenda. In short, Correa, because of reasons that include the most fortunate financial circumstances, has amassed a level of power has put the future of Ecuadorian democracy in peril.

The relationships of financial circumstances and the outcome of major events are very palpable throughout Ecuadorian history. But this is clearly a worldwide phenomenon. Time and time again throughout historical events, historians are able to track down the reasons for major sociopolitical events to economic matters. For example, it is understood that the United States delayed abolishing slavery because of the financial implications such a move would have had in the cotton industry. And in

---

[227] *Indices económicos del Ecuador. Country Statistics.*

the modern world, revolutions are affected by the financial context. The legalization of marijuana, for instance, is persistently supported due to the vast amounts of tax revenue that such a policy would bring. More significantly, a revolution to save our natural environment is only beginning to be made possible due to the financial markets it is creating. In Ecuador, finances have undoubtedly been key; around the world, well, money makes it go round.

Appendix

Table 3-A: Primary education 1902-1928[228]

Year	Schools	Enrollment	Attendance
1902	1,317	83,648	--
1909	1,355	85,237	--
1914	1,411	86,981	--
1915	1,231	95,091	--
1916	1,400	97,395	85,241
1919	1,630	99,254	85,014
1921	1,716	103,344	89,895
1924	1,488	112,219	101,376
1928	1,771	128,746	111,699

Table 12-A: Market value of the sucre in New York 1920-1926 in US dollars[229]

Year	Value	Year	Value
1920	0.44	1924	0.20
1921	0.28	1925	0.23
1922	0.26	1926	0.20
1923	0.21		

[228] Sources: Rodriguez, *Government Finances and the Search for Public Policy*, 91. Ecuadorian Ministerio de Educación.

[229] Rodriguez, *Government Finances and the Search for Public Policy*, 147.

Table 37-A: Petroleum derivatives exports, 1972-2000[183]

Year	Amount in US dollars (FOB) x 1000	Year	Amount in US dollars (FOB) x 1000
1972	448	1987	78,215
1973	689	1988	101,606
1974	3,951	1989	114,742
1975	-	1990	150,234
1976	1,637	1991	93,125
1977	15,827	1992	85,730
1978	91,380	1993	104,509
1979	145,418	1994	119,794
1980	192,659	1995	134,457
1981	166,534	1996	227,859
1982	136,904	1997	145,689
1983	101,041	1998	133,970
1984	156,400	1999	167,371
1985	101,917	2000	198,415
1986	70,114		

Supplements

Supplement A

Main Peruvian mobilizations towards Ecuadorian territory prior to 1941[230].

February 1935: A Peruvian detachment party advanced from the mouth of the Curaray river to Puerto Nashiño, located in front of the Ecuadorian detachment of Tarqui. Approximate advance: 180 km over the Curaray river.

October 1935: Peruvian detachment parties advanced from the mouth of the Morona river in the Marañón, to the Alto Morona, point in which the river is no longer navigable, at a distance of 18km to the Ecuadorian garrison. Approximate advance: 200km over the Morona river.

February 1936: The Peruvian garrison of Puerto Arana, in the Tigre river, advanced until Puerto Bartra, head to head with the Ecuadorian garrison González Suárez. Approximate advance: 260km over the Tigre river.

September 1936: Peruvian detachment parties advanced from Puerto Borja (Ecuadorian territory where a civil authority had recently been displaced) to Puerto Meléndez (Peruvian), on the mouth of the Santiago river on the Marañón. Approximate advance: 70km.

May 1938: Peruvian advance from Teniente Pingle on the Santiago river, to the Vargas Guerra garrison on the Morona river. Approximate advance 85Km.

June 1938: The Peruvian Garrison of Soplin, situated in front of the Ecuadorian garrison of Huachi, on the Pastaza river, advanced until it joined the Vargas Guerra garrison in Morona.

---

230 Jorge Villacres Moscoso, *Problemas económicos y políticos del Ecuador*, vol. 1 (Guayaquil: ESPOL, 1978), 108.

June 1938: Peruvian detachments attacked the Ecuadorian garrison stationed at Puerto Cisneros in the Huasaga river.

September 1940: Peruvian detachments stationed in Nupatacaini, on the Marañón river, build a gauge northeast to the Zamora river, stationing them in front of the Ecuadorian garrison of Cumbariza, situated at a distance of 30km of the village of Zamora. Approximate advance: 130km.

October 1940: The Peruvian detachment of Cabo Reyes, on the Santiago river advanced to the Zamora river, and into the Nangariza river eluding the Cordillera del Cóndor and trying to penetrate the vicinity of Gualaquiza and Zamora. Approximate distance covered by this advance: 45Km.

Supplement B: List of Presidents of Ecuador: 1895-2002

Years in Office	Name	Party	Notes
2007 – 2017 (expected)	Rafael Correa	Alianza PAIS	
2005 - 2007	Alfredo Palacio		No official affiliation.
2002 - 2005	Lucio Gutiérrez	Partido Sociedad Patriótica (PSP)	Interrupted presidency.
2000 - 2002	Gustavo Noboa	Democracia Popular - Unión Demócrata Cristiana (DP-UDC)	Mahuad's vice-president, assumed office after he was overthrown.
2000	Gen. Carlos Mendoza Poveda Carlos Antonio Vargas Carlos Solórzano		Military Junta.
2000	Col. Lucio Gutiérrez Borbúa Carlos Antonio Vargas Carlos Solórzano		"National Salvation Government" Junta
1998 - 2000	Jamil Mahuad	Democracia Popular - Unión Demócrata Cristiana (DP-UDC)	Interrupted presidency after coup d' état.
1997 - 1998	Fabián Alarcón	Frente Radical Alfarista	Interim President.
1997	Rosalía Arteaga Serrano	Movimiento Independiente por una República Auténtica (MIRA)	Bucaram's vice president, assumed office after he was overthrown. She served for two days.
1997	Fabián Alarcón	Frente Radical Alfarista	Interim President.
1996 - 1997	Abdalá Bucaram Ortíz	Partido Roldosista Ecuatoriano (PRE)	Overthrown after he was deemed unfit to rule.
1992 - 1996	Sixto Durán-	Partido Unidad	

	Ballén Córdovez	Republicana (PUR)	
1988 - 1992	Rodrigo Borja Cevallos	Izquierda Democrática (ID)	
1984 - 1988	León Febres Cordero	Frente de Reconstrucción Nacional (FRN)	
1981 - 1984	Osvaldo Hurtado Larrea	Democracia Popular - Unión Demócrata Cristiana (DP-UDC)	Assumed the presidency in 1981 after the death of President Roldós.
1979 - 1981	Jaime Roldós Aguilera	Concentración de Fuerzas Populares (CFP)	
1976-1979	Admr. Alfredo Poveda Burbano Gen. Luis Leoro Franco Gen. Guillermo Durán Arcentales		Military Junta.
1972-1976	Guillermo Rodríguez Lara		Military dictator.
1968-1972	José María Velasco Ibarra	Frente Nacional Velasquista (FNV)	
1966-1968	Otto Arosemena Gómez	Coalición Institucional Democrática (CID)	Interim President.
1966	Clemente Yerovi Indaburu		Interim President.
1966	Gen. Telmo O. Vargas B.		Jefe de Estado
1963-1966	Admr. Ramón Castro Jijón Gen. Luis Cabrera Sevilla Col. Guillermo Freile		Military Junta

	Posso Gen. Mario Gándara Enríquez		
1961-1963	Carlos Julio Arosemena Monroy	Frente Nacional Velasquista (FNV)	
1960-1961	José María Velasco Ibarra	Frente Nacional Velasquista (FNV)	
1956-1960	Camilo Ponce Enríquez	Movimiento Social Cristiano (MSC)	
1952-1956	José María Velasco Ibarra		
1948-1952	Galo Plaza Lasso	Movimiento Cívico Democrático Nacional (MCDN)	
1947-1948	Carlos Julio Arosemena Tola		
1947	Mariano Suárez Veintimilla	Partido Conservador Ecuatoriano (PCE)	Provisional President.
1947	Col. Carlos Mancheno Cajas		Interim President.
1944-1947	José María Velasco Ibarra	Alianza Democrática (AD)	Constitutional President.
1944	José María Velasco Ibarra		Interim President.
1940-1944	Carlos Alberto Arroyo del Río		Constitutional President.
1940	Julio Enrique Moreno Peñaherrera		President of the Senate. Interim President.
1939-1940	Andrés F. Córdoba		Interim President.
1939	Manuel María Borrero González		Interim President.
1939	Carlos Alberto Arroyo del Río		President of the Senate. Interim President.

1938-1939	Aurelio Mosquera Narváez	Constitutional President
1937-1938	Gil Alberto Enríquez Gallo	Jefe Supremo
1935-1937	Antonio Pons Campusano	Minister of Government - Interim President.
1934-1935	José María Velasco Ibarra	Constitutional President
1932-1933	Juan de Dios Martínez Mera	Constitutional President
1932	Alberto Guerrero Martínez	President of the Senate - Interim President.
1932	Carlos Freile Larrea	Minister of Government - Interim President.
1931-1932	Alfredo Baquerizo Moreno	President of the Senate - Interim President.
1931	Luis Alberto Larrea Alba	Minister of Government - Interim President.
1929-1931	Isidro Ayora Cueva	Constitutional President
1926	Isidro Ayora Cueva	
1926	Julio E. Moreno Homero Viteri Lafronte Isidro Ayora Humberto Albornoz Adolfo Hidalgo Narváez José A. Gómez Gault	Provisional Government Junta.
1925-1926	Rafael Bustamante Luis N. Dillon Francisco Gómez de la Torre Pedro Pablo Garaicoa Francisco J. Bolona Francisco Arízaga Luque	Provisional Government Junta.
1924-1925	Gonzalo S.	

	Córdoba	
1920-1924	José Luis Tamayo Terán	
1916-1920	Alfredo Baquerizo Moreno	
1912-1916	Leónidas Plaza Gutiérrez	
1912	Francisco Higinio Andreade Marín y Rivadeneira	Interim President.
1911-1912	Carlos Freile Zaldumbide	Interim President.
1911	Pedro J. Montero	Jefe Supremo
1911	Flavio Alfaro	Jefe Supremo
1911	Emilio Estrada y Carmona	
1911	Carlos Freile Zaldumbide	Interim President.
1907-1911	José Eloy Alfaro Delgado	
1906-1907	José Eloy Alfaro Delgado	Interim President.
1906	José Eloy Alfaro Delgado	Jefe Supremo
1905-1906	Lizardo García Sorroza	
1901-1905	Leonidas Plaza	
1895-1901	José Eloy Alfaro Delgado	Jefe Supremo (June 5, 1895 - October 9, 1896) Interim President (October 9, 1896 - January 17, 1897) President (January 17, 1897 - August 31, 1901)

Supplement C: Timeline of Important Events

Year	Event
1895	Start of the Liberal Era
1908	Quito - Guayaquil railroad completed
1910	Conflict with Peru begins period overspending
1912	Eloy Alfaro is murdered after ruling for 11 years
1914	Apex of cacao bonanza, 77.3% of total country exports
1915	Public debt begins to exponentially increase
1917	Ecuador loses its place as the world's leading producer of cacao
1918	Sanitation of Guayaquil completed
1925	Julian Revolution
1926	Kemmerer arrives in Ecuador to organize a post-cacao economy
1929	Stock market crash of 1929 impacts Ecuador
1930	Student revolt marks the beginning of a period of continuous struggle
1931	Indigenous uprising
1932	Indigenous uprising
1933	Indigenous uprising
1934	Indigenous uprising
1941	Ecuador goes to war with Peru
1942	Ecuador signs Rio de Janeiro protocol
1945	WWII ends and the banana bonanza begins in Ecuador
1948	Galo Plaza is elected president and Ecuador becomes the premier banana exporter
1963	Banana production suffers
1966	Banana production recovers
1967	Texaco-Gulf consortium strikes oil at Lago Agrio
1972	Oil pipeline is completed and oil boom begins in Ecuador
1972	Military takes a hold of power
1974	Fast GDP growth begins and is accompanied by massive debt accumulation
1979	Military ends rule leaving the country with immense debt
1981	Oil revenue suffers and state budgets are covered with increasing debt
1992	Sixto Durán Ballén is elected president and begins a period of

Year	Event
	globalization
1995	Ecuador signs its adhesion to the WTO
1998	Oil prices hit all time low
1998	Peace treaty is signed with Peru
1998	Financial crisis begins
2000	El Niño wreaks havoc in Ecuador
2000	Dollarization is put into effect to combat skyrocketing inflation
2000	President Mahuad is deposed

Bibliography & Sources

Works Cited

Academia nacional de historia militar, comp. *Historia militar del Ecuador.* Edited by David Andrade. 1st ed. Quito: Ministerio De Defensa Nacional Del Ecuador, 2010.

"Bananas US Ports." *Global Financial Database.* Accessed June 27, 2012. https://www.globalfinancialdata.com/.

Banco Central del Ecuador. *Indices económicos del Ecuador.* Country Statistics. Accessed February 1, 2012. https://www.bce.fin.ec/documentos/PublicacionesNotas/Catalogo/Anuario/80anios/indice.htm.

Dobronski, Fernando. *El Ecuador: Los hechos más importantes de su historia.* Quito: Soboc Grafic, 2003.

Drake, Paul W. *Kemmerer En Los Andes: La misión Kemmerer: 1923-1933.* Quito: Banco Central Del Ecuador, 1995.

El Tiempo (Quito). "Problemas fiscales y laborales afronta el gobierno interino." November 30, 1966.

Gerlach, Allen. *Indians, Oil, and Politics: A Recent History of Ecuador.* Wilmington, DE: Scholarly Resources, 2003.

Global Financial Data "West Texas Intermediate Oil Price (US$/Barrel).". Accessed August 17, 2012. http://www.globalfinancialdata.com/.

Henderson, Paul. "Cocoa, Finance and the State in Ecuador, 1895-1925." *Bulletin of Latin American Research* 16 (1997): 169-186. Accessed August 31, 2011. http://www.jstor.org/stable/3339105.

Lahmeyer, Jan. "Ecuador: Population Growth of the Whole Country." ECUADOR: Population Growth of the Whole Country. April 4, 2003. Accessed June 27, 2012. http://www.populstat.info/Americas/ecuadorc.htm.

Lahmeyer, Jan. "Ecuador: Urban Population." Ecuador: Urban Population. Accessed August 5, 2012. http://www.populstat.info/Americas/ecuadort.htm.

Maddison, Angus. *Historical Statistics of the World Economy: 1-2008 AD.* Historical Statistics Report. Accessed June 17, 2012. www.ggdc.net Published by The Groningen Growth and Development Centre.

May, Stacy, and Galo Plaza Lasso. *The United Fruit Company in Latin America.* New York: Arno Press, 1976.

Parsons, James J. "Bananas in Ecuador: A New Chapter in the History of Tropical Agriculture." *Economic Geography* 33, no. 3 (July 1957): 201-16. Accessed June 17, 2012. http://www.jstor.org/stable/142308.

Peñaherrera, Blasco. *Historia del Ecuador.* Edited by Ricardo Martín. Barcelona: Salvat Editores, 1980.

Pineo, Ronn. *Ecuador and the United States Useful Strangers (The United States and the Americas).* New York: University of Georgia Press, 2007.

Rodríguez, Linda Alexander. *The Search for Public Policy: Regional Politics and Government Finances in Ecuador, 1830-1940.* Berkeley: University of California Press, 1985.

Striffler, Steve. *In the Shadows of State and Capital: The United Fruit Company, Popular Struggle, and Agrarian Restructuring in Ecuador, 1900-1995.* Durham, NC: Duke University Press, 2002.

United States of America. Department of State. Office of the Historian. *Editorial Note.* Vol. V. Series 306. Department of State. Accessed July 17, 2011. http://history.state.gov/historicaldocuments/frus1958-60v05/d306.

United States of America. Department of State. Office of the Historian. *Memorandum of a Conversation, Department of State, Washington, August 31, 1955.* Accessed July 17, 2011. http://history.state.gov/historicaldocuments/frus1955-57v07/d471.

World Bank "Data: Ecuador.". Accessed August 17, 2012. http://data.worldbank.org/country/ecuador.

World Bank "World DataBank." Accessed August 14, 2012. http://databank.worldbank.org/data/home.aspx.

Vergara, Alfredo. *América Latina, entre sombras y luces.* Quito, Ecuador:

Paradiso Editores, 2003.

Villacres Moscoso, Jorge. *Problemas economicos y políticos del Ecuador.* Vol. 1. Guayaquil: ESPOL, 1978.

Archives

Central Bank of Ecuador, Quito

Ministry of Foreign Relations, Quito

Private collection of documents: Homero Andrade Alcivar, Chone

United States Department of State, Washington D.C.

Published works and other sources

Academia nacional de historia militar, comp. *Historia militar del Ecuador.* Edited by David Andrade. 1st ed. Quito: Ministerio De Defensa Nacional Del Ecuador, 2010.

Provides a focus on the events concerning the Ecuadorian military within Ecuadorian history.

Acosta, Alberto. *Breve historia económica del Ecuador.* Quito: Corporación Editora Nacional, 2002.

Ecuador's Economic history, it provides a valuable point of view of the economical circumstances of the country.

Acosta, Alberto. *La deuda eterna: una historia de la deuda externa ecuatoriana.* [Quito]: Ed. El Duende, 1990.

A history of the Ecuadorian foreign debt until 1990.

Acostoa E., Alberto, Magdalena Aguilar Aguilar, Carlos E. Quevedo T., Walter Spurrier Baquerizo, and Cornelio Marchán. *Ecuador: petróleo y crisis econónmica.* Quito: Instituto Latinoamericano De Investigaciones Sociales, 1986.

Source on the impact of oil in Ecuador.

Aguirre, Manuel Agustin, Leonicio Gustavo Cevallos, Rafael Alfonso Procel C., Milton Mejia Yepez, Celso Jimenez S., and Segundo R. Viteri E. *Boletin trimestral de informacion económica.* Quito: Instituto De Investigaciones Economicas De La Universidad Central, 1954.

Gives a deatiled account of the financial situation of Ecuador in 1954. Most importantly, it provides a background connection to 1954 through a historical argument. Details of Ecuador´s main products like Cacao (Ecuador´s main export at the time) are quite useful in determining the Economic environment of the time.

Almeida, Guzmán Patricio., and Arroba Rebeca. Almeida. *Estadíticas económicas históricas 1948-1983.* Quito: Banco Central Del Ecuador, 1988.

35 years of Ecuadorian economic statistics.

Arosemena, Guillermo. *La historia empresarial del Ecuador.* Guayaquil: S.N., 1995.

Provides the development of the corporate world in Ecuador. It is interesting to note the correlations between the creation of these with the major events in society and politics.

Arosemena, Guillermo. *La revitalización de la economía Ecuatoriana: los hechos, las causas, los males y las soluciones.* Guayaquil: S.N., 1993.

An economic history of Ecuador with its causes and effects.

Banco Central del Ecuador. *Indices económicos del Ecuador.* Country Statistics. Accessed February 1, 2012. https://www.bce.fin.ec/documentos/PublicacionesNotas/Catalogo/Anuario/80anios/indice.htm.

Country Statistics published by the Central Bank of Ecuador

Betancourt, Roberto, Cristian Espinosa, Juan Falconi, Patricio Izurieta Mora Bowen, Patricio Leon, Alfonso Lopez, Salvador Marconi, and Antonio Rodas. *El Ecuador frente alLa Organización Mundial de Comercio.* Quito: Banco Central Del Ecuador, 1996.

Báez, René. *Ecuador: ¿Genocidio económico o vía democrática.* Quito: Corporación Ed. Nacional, 1992.

Bucheli, Marcelo. *Bananas and Business: The United Fruit Company in Colombia, 1899-2000.* New York: New York University Press, 2005.

Includes statistics on the Banana trade that are relevant to the Ecuadorian issue.

Cambridge Economic History of Latin America. New York, NY: Cambridge University Press, 2006.

A history of other nations in South America is useful for comparison purposes.

Canessa, Mario. *La banca del Ecuador: una explicación histórica.* Guayaquil: ESPOL, 1999.

A history of the role of banks in the Ecuadorian economy.

Carbo, Luis Alberto. *Historia monetaria y cambiaria del Ecuador.* Quito: Central Bank of Ecuador, 1978.

Chapters XXIII to XXXIV. These chapters offer a monetary history from the end WWI to 1953.

A great financial background for a time period where two significant events in Ecuadorian history took place (The Julian Revolutionn and the war with Peru).

"Carta Dirigida Al BID Por La Secretaria General Del Gobierno Del Ecuador." Letter to Gustavo Larrea Cordoba—Ecuadorian Ambassador in Washington D.C. December 30, 1965. Historical Archive of the Ministry of Foreign Relations of Ecuador, Quito, Ecuador.

This previously classified letter demonstrates important issues of the time. Particularly, with regards to Washington.

Casals, Juan. *Incidencia del banco central del Ecuador en la historia económica y social del país y del exterior.* Quito: S.N., 2003.

The Central Bank of Ecuador is historically an important part of the economy and its history proves useful when analyzing economic change.

Chomsky, Noam, Denise Glasbeek, Julian Sempill, and Heinz Dieterich. *Latin America From Colonization to Globalization.* New York: Ocean Press, 1999.

"CIA - The World Factbook." Welcome to the CIA Web Site — Central Intelligence Agency. Accessed September 01, 2011. https://www.cia.gov/library/publications/the-world-factbook/geos/ec.html.

Main financial indicators are found in this database.

Correa Paredes, Julio. *La economía de La República.* Vol. 7. Quito: Ministerio De Relaciones Exteriores, 1982.

Summary of the Economic situation of Ecuador during part of the 20th century. Most interestingly, provides the financial problems leading to the 1941 conflict with Peru.

Corsino, Cárdenas José. *Ensayo histórico de la economía ecuatoriana.* Quito: Ed. Del Banco Central Del Ecuador, 1995.

Historical essay of the Ecuadorian economy.

Córdova, Gabriela. *Anatomía de los golpes de estado: la prensa en la caída de Mahuad Y Bucaram.* Quito: Universidad Andina Simón Bolívar, Ecuador, 2003.

Talks about the role of the press in the coup d'états of Bucaram and Mahuad. This provides a framework for comparing influences of this kind with financial ones.

"Data: Ecuador." The World Bank. Accessed August 17, 2012. http://data.worldbank.org/country/ecuador.

Dobronski, Fernando. *El Ecuador: los hechos más importantes de su historia.* Quito: Soboc Grafic, 2003.

A brief history of Ecuador, this title outlines the major events of Ecuadorian history.

Drake, Paul W. *Kemmerer en los Andes: la misión Kemmerer: 1923-1933.* Quito: Banco Central Del Ecuador, 1995.

Kemmerer provided Latin America with the tools to implement the desired economic policy of the time. His team had a profound impact on the way the Latin American Eocnomies (including Ecuador) functioned. Consequently, this literature provides an in depth look into the causes for the performance of the Ecuadorian economy during that time.

Ecuador. Ministerio De Relaciones Exteriores. Dirección General De Tratados. *Memoria histórica de los tratados bilaterales y regionales suscritos por la República del Ecuador De 1830 Al 2009.* Vol. IX - XVIII. Quito, 2009.

A catalog containing most treaties signed by the Republic of Ecuador.

El Tiempo (Quito). "Problemas fiscales y laborales afronta el gobierno interino." November 30, 1966.

Falconi, Juan, Patricio Leon, and Julio Oleas Montalvo. *Setenta años del Banco Central Del Ecuador: pasado, presente y proyección al futuro.* Quito: Banco Central Del Ecuador, 1997.

The Central Bank of Ecuador is historically an important part of the economy and its history proves useful when analyzing economic change.

Ferguson, Niall. "Revolution outside Britain." Lecture, Harvard University, Cambridge, Massachusetts, 2010.

Fierro Carrión, Luis. *Los grupos financieros en el Ecuador.* Quito: CEDEP, Centro De Educación Popular, 1992.

Provides an overview of the financial groups in Ecuador. It is particularly interesting to create a connection between these interest groups and the financial effects they caused.

Fischer, Sabine. *Estado, Clases E Industria: La Emergencia Del Capitalismo Ecuatoriano Y Los Intereses Azucareros.*

A look into capitalist Ecuador. Provides bases for comparison with major events.

Gerlach, Allen. *Indians, Oil, and Politics: A Recent History of Ecuador.* Wilmington, DE: Scholarly Resources, 2003.

Provides a history of 20th century Ecuador from an international author's perspective.

Global Financial Database "Bananas US Ports.". Accessed June 27, 2012. https://www.globalfinancialdata.com/.

Henderson, Paul. "Cocoa, Finance and the State in Ecuador, 1895-1925." *Bulletin of Latin American Research* 16 (1997): 169-186. Accessed August 31, 2011. http://www.jstor.org/stable/3339105.

Published by: Blackwell Publishing on behalf of Society for Latin American Studies. Newsletter addressing the Cocoa industry in Ecuador, 1895-1925. It references some of the other sources on the bibliography.

Kohan, R. M. *Economic and Financial Conditions in Ecuador.* Report. London: Majesty's Stationery Office, 1928.

Publication of the Department of Oversees Trade. It provides the point of view of the economic situations in Ecuador in 1928. It is particularly significant because it gives the perspective of a world power in that point in time as opposed to the self observation of Ecuadorian sources.

Kymlicka, Will. *Multicultural Citizenship A Liberal Theory of Minority Rights (Oxford Political Theory).* New York: Oxford University Press, USA, 1996.

Lahmeyer, Jan. "Ecuador: Population Growth of the Whole Country." Ecuador: Population Growth of the Whole Country. April 4, 2003. Accessed June 27, 2012. http://www.populstat.info/Americas/ecuadorc.htm.

Lahmeyer, Jan. "Ecuador: Urban Population." Ecuador: Urban Population. Accessed August 5, 2012. http://www.populstat.info/Americas/ecuadort.htm.

Larrea Stacey, Eduardo. *Evolución de la política del Banco Central del Ecuador 1927-1987.*

Being, perhaps, the most important economics institution in 20th century Ecuador. It is necessary to look at the shifts in its economic policy so as to understand the performance of the economy.

London, H. Stanford. *Economic and Financial Conditions in Ecuador.* Report. London: His Majesty's Stationery Office, 1934.

Publication of the Department of Oversees Trade. It provides the point of view of the economic situations in Ecuador in 1934. It is particularly significant because it gives the perspective of a world power in that point in time as opposed to the self observation of Ecuadorian sources.

Maddison, Angus. *Historical Statistics of the World Economy: 1-2008 AD.* Historical Statistics Report. Accessed June 17, 2012. www.ggdc.net Published by The Groningen Growth and Development Centre.

Marchán, R. Carlos. *La banca central en el entorno de la crisis financiera del Ecuador: (factores Que La Originan Y Son Causa De Su Profundización, 1995-1999) / Carlos Marchán Romero.* Quito, Ecuador: Banco Central Del Ecuador, 2005.

An in depth look in to the financial crisis of the late 1990s.

May, Stacy, and Galo Plaza Lasso. *The United Fruit Company in Latin America.* New York: Arno Press, 1976.

Merchan, Carlos. *Historia del Banco CentraldDel Ecuador: de banco de gobierno a banco emisor y vuelta al pasado, 1927-2000.* Quito: Banco Central Del Ecuador, 2005.

The Central Bank of Ecuador is historically an important part of the economy and its history proves useful when analyzing economic change.

Mino, Wilson. La crisis de los treinta y sus repercusiones monetarias: 1927-1932. Quito: Banco Central Del Ecuador, 1988.

A look into the crisis following the Julian Revolution.

Naranjo, C., P. Marco, Miguel Acosta, Ivan Gachet, and Ivan E. Las constituyentes y el sistema económico del Ecuador. Quito: Banco Central Ecuador, 2007.

Provides the constitutions of Ecuador and their correspondent economic models. Very useful for analysis of economic organization and the type of events that arise from them.

Offerdal, Erik, Mariano Cortés, Mayra Zermeño, Alvin Hilaire, Gabriela Inchauste, Fernando Delgado, Antonio Pancorbo, and Werner Keller. Ecuador: Selected Issues and Statistical Annex. Report no. 00/125. Washington D.C.: International Monetary Fund, 2000.

Ojeda, Galo Abril. Política monetaria y desarrollo industrial en el Ecuador (1970-1983). Vol. 11. Quito: Banco Central Del Ecuador, 1985.

An analysis of the effects of monetary policy in the Ecuadorian economy it provides a window into the actions that had an effect on the economy that influenced ecuadorian events.

Ortiz, Gonzalo. Resumen de la historia económica del Ecuador, Siglo XX. Quito, Ecuador: Abya-Yala, 2000.

A brief history of the economic conditions in Ecuador.

Parker, David Hanson. Political Decision Making in Ecuador: The Influence of Business Groups. Diss., University of Florida, 1972. Michigan: UMI Dissertation Information Service, 1972.

A source that provides a look into the influence of business groups.

Parsons, James J. "Bananas in Ecuador: A New Chapter in the History of Tropical Agriculture." Economic Geography 33, no. 3 (July 1957): 201-16. Accessed June 17, 2012.

http://www.jstor.org/stable/142308.

Peñaherrera, Blasco. Historia Del Ecuador. Edited by Ricardo Martín. Barcelona: Salvat Editores, 1980.

Pineo, Ronn. Ecuador and the United States Useful Strangers (The United States and the Americas). New York: University of Georgia Press, 2007.

Very useful book about the relationship between the United States of America and Ecuador. It provides an analysis of how the economic circumstances and the relationship with the United States played such an important role in Ecuadorian history.

Pérez, Chiriboga Guillermo, and Wilson Miño. Pensamiento económico. Quito: Banco Central Del Ecuador, 1997.

Provides a history of economic thought among ecuadorian economists. This is interesting as it is possible to relate economic thought to economic policy.

"Reaccion del departamento de estado ante declaración de nulidad del Protocolo De Rio." Letter to Enrique Sanchez Baron. September 21, 1960. Historic Archive of the Ministry of Foreign Relation, Quito, Ecuador.

This previously classified letter depicts the focus of the Ecuadorian government at the time.

Rodríguez, Linda Alexander. The Search for Public Policy: Regional Politics and Government Finances in Ecuador, 1830-1940. Berkeley: University of California Press, 1985.

Samaniego Ponce, José. crisis económica del Ecuador: análisis comparativo de dos períodos históricos: (1929 - 1933) - (1980 - 1984). Quito: Banco Central Del Ecuador, 1988.

Comparitive Anayisis of economic crises in Ecuador.

Setenta años de información estadística. Quito: Banco Central Del Ecuador, 1997.

70 years of Ecuadorian financial indicators.

Striffler, Steve. In the Shadows of State and Capital: The United Fruit Company, Popular Struggle, and Agrarian Restructuring in Ecuador, 1900-1995. Durham, NC: Duke University Press, 2002.

Provides a history of very important aspects of Ecuadorian economic history. Particularly interesting with regards to our subject matter in this literature is the focus given to agrarian reform.

Thorp, Rosemary. Las crisis en el Ecuador: los treinta y ochenta. Quito: Corp. Ed. Nacional, 1991.

A look into the crises of the 1930's and 1980's in Ecuador. A valuable starting point for investigating the financial impact on major events.

Thorp, Rosemary. Progreso, Pobreza y exclusion una historia economica de América Latina en el siglo XX. Banco Interamericano de Desarrollo, 1998.

As in other histories of Latin America, it is useful to look at examples of other nations so as to compare with Ecuador.

United States of America. Department of State. Office of the Historian. Circular Airgram From the Secretary of State to Certain Diplomatic Missions. Vol. VII. Series 487. Accessed July 17, 2011. http://history.state.gov/historicaldocuments/frus1955-57v07/d487.

United States of America. Department of State. Office of the Historian. Editorial Note. Vol. V. Series 306. Department of State. Accessed July 17, 2011. http://history.state.gov/historicaldocuments/frus1958-60v05/d306.

Particularly notable is Nixon's assertion that "the need to resolve the area's economic problems as a prerequisite to curing the political problems".

United States of America. Department of State. Office of the Historian. Letter From the Ambassador in Brazil (Briggs) to the Assistant Secretary of State for Inter-American Affairs (Holland). By Ellis Briggs. Accessed July 17, 2011. http://history.state.gov/historicaldocuments/frus1955-57v07/d521.

The opinion of "divid[ing] Ecuador between Peru & Colombia" is made by an American ambassador. Shows that perhaps the main concern from the United States was economic growth.

United States of America. Department of State. Office of the Historian. Memorandum of a Conversation, Department of State, Washington, August 31, 1955. Accessed July 17, 2011. http://history.state.gov/historicaldocuments/frus1955-57v07/d471.

Discusses Ecuador's desperation for Eximbank loan.

Vergara, Alfredo. *América Latina, entre sombras y luces.* Quito, Ecuador: Paradiso Editores, 2003.

A straightforward book of what happened in Ecuador and Latin America's economies. Particular emphasis is given to debt and the causes for said debt.

Villacres Moscoso, Jorge. *Problemas económicos y políticos del Ecuador.* Vol. 1. Guayaquil: ESPOL, 1978.

Book encompassing various conferences given by Dr. Jorge Villacres Moscoso. It outlines, with a reference to important historical facts, the important economic and political situations of the time.

Villacres Moscoso, Jorge W. "La política financiera internacional del Ecuador durante la primera mitad del siglo XX." In *La política comercial y financiera internacional del Ecuador,* 187-222. Guayaquil: Universidad De Guayaquil, 1959.

Gives a detailed summary of Ecuador's international commercial and financial policy of the first half of the 20th century.

Winn, Peter, Paul W. Drake, Volker K. Frank, Joel Stillerman, and Rachel Schurman. *Victims of the Chilean Miracle: Workers and Neoliberalism in the Pinochet Era, 1973–2002.* Duke University Press, 2004.

World Bank "World DataBank.". Accessed August 14, 2012. http://databank.worldbank.org/data/home.aspx.

Index

www.ingramcontent.com/pod-product-compliance
Lightning Source LLC
Chambersburg PA
CBHW071246180926
51613CB00006B/264/J
9781622734702